The Definitive Guide to

Brighton's Best Pubs

An A-Z of every pub in Brighton,
independently rated

- The Pub Jury -

This edition printed June 2006

For updates, information, enquiries:
brightonpubs@yahoo.co.uk

or check out the website:
www.pubjury.co.uk

or the blog:
http://brightonpubs.blogspot.com/

A CIP catalogue record for this book is available from the British Library

First published in Great Britain by
Pen Press Publishers Ltd
The Old School Road
39 Chesham Road
Brighton BN2 1NB

ISBN 10: 1-905621-39-6
ISBN 13: 978-1-905621-39-2

Disclaimer: The scores and the descriptions given for the pubs are those determined by the jurors at the time of visiting. The publisher, editor and author of this book are not liable for any inaccuracies or insulting comments contained therein. If you feel something is inaccurate, please email us and the pub will be re-visited and the points addressed.

Thank you to Harveys of Lewes for their assistance

Also thanks to Janette, Tim, Richard, Attila, Iain, Jonathan, Dave B, Dave E, Dave R, Jennifer, Sandra, Adrian, Vinni, Mick, Matt, Geoff, Ollie, & Scottish John, for your research, assistance and limitless patience when I kept going on about this project

FOREWORD

By Attila the Stockbroker

Well done to Tony and cohorts for getting (probably 'staggering' is a better word given the subject matter!) off their arses and producing this exhaustive guide to the drinking delights of the most exciting city in the UK. There are pubs to suit all tastes in Brighton, and most people have their favourite. Mine is celebrated in the poem below. Cheers everyone!

Attila

This poem is dedicated to everyone at the Evening Star in Surrey Street, in my opinion the best pub in the WORLD! The poem celebrates the wonderful concoctions of its parent brewery, the Dark Star Brewing Company. I have been drinking – and occasionally gigging – there since 1992, and to be honest, although I happily go all over Brighton watching bands at many different venues, if I just want a drink, I wouldn't even think of going anywhere else. Furthermore, the beer at some – not all - of the town's music venues can only be described as the urine of Satan, and therefore I will very often drink my fill in the Star so I am happily lubricated before I head off to the gig...)

BEER GARDENING

Come into the Beer Garden!
It's not very far.
What's that light that points the way?
It's the Evening Star.
We all love Beer Gardening
As the sun goes down.
Who's that crashed out on the floor?
InCapability Brown.

Come into the Beer Garden
Through the Golden Gate!
Sunburst makes your Hophead swim -
Meltdown seals your fate...
Pees, then Leeks, then Sycamore.
Got to let it go!
What's that in the Yucca Plant?
You don't want to know....

Four hours in the Beer Garden -
God, I need a kip.
Insects are all outsects now.
Flies have got no zip.
Stagger onto the last train.
Cuddle up in bed.
Red Hot Poker's lost his poke.
Shrimp Plant's there instead.

ATTILA THE STOCKBROKER

www.attilathestockbroker.com
www.myspace.com/attilastockbroker

BBP

CONTENTS

THE BASICS 7
- Introduction: The Best Pub 8
- Brighton 8
- The System 9
- Juror Portraits 11

THE VERDICT 13
- Brighton's Best Pubs: The Top Ten 14
- The Different Areas of Brighton 16
- Best Speciality Pubs 21

THE A-Z 27
- The Maps 28
- The A-Z of all 300 pubs & bars 36

THE FUN 159
- Pub Crawls 160
- Pub Drinking Games 164

THE CLUBS 167
- Brighton Club Guide 168

THE REST 173
- Local Breweries and Beers 174
- Local Pub Chains 178
- Pub Graveyard 181
- Updates 183
- Disclaimer 183

THE DISTRACTIONS 185
- Boys Night Out Application Form 186
- Pub Humour 187
- Puzzles 202

THE BASICS

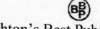

Brighton's Best Pubs: The Basics

Introduction: The Best Pub

The best pub is a welcoming place, a home from home, with a roaring fire in the winter, a smiling barmaid or friendly barman, various distractions to entertain you, or a calm haven or refuge to escape the rigours of the modern world. It's full of familiar faces, background laughter, ready with a foaming pint of the finest real ale, a perfectly chilled lager or a wide range of whiskies. There is a garden fringed with flowers in bloom, a room with comfortable sofas, a smooth wooden floor and a long bar to lean against. There is music when you want it and quiet when you don't, games or newspapers, quizzes or bands. It's a place to watch your favourite team play, chase the opposite sex or just plain get drunk. The best pub is one thing to one person and another to another. The best pub varies depending on your mood and the day of the week.

British pubs are a unique part of the culture on our islands. They are something that is appealing to visitors and badly missed by Brits abroad. How do you quantify how good a pub is so that someone else knows what to expect?

This book is based on a system that has evolved over the past few years in an attempt to rate pubs to determine just how good they are and which of them is the Best. It isn't perfect, because rating pubs is a very personal experience and sometimes it is just not possible to say what is so good about a place where you feel happy and at home. But we think we've had a good go at it and we hope you will agree.

Brighton

What better place to go drinking than Brighton? Newly a city, gradually transforming itself from a pleasant seaside town to an exciting metropolis, with a glorious micro-climate making it the Algarve of England. Known as a miniature London-by-the-sea for the cultural mix and wide entertainment available, but with friendly locals and manageable size.

Sources say that there are over 400 places to get a drink in Brighton and judging from the heavy research undertaken to complete this book, they are probably right.

This book covers every pub and bar in Brighton, Hove, Kemptown and Hanover. There is also a section on nightclubs. Hotel bars are only covered if they actively encourage non-residents to drink there. No restaurants or places where you have to eat to be able to drink – you've got to draw the line somewhere! This area spans from the Western line of Sackville Road on the Hove/Portslade border over to the East at the Marina, to the Northern boundary of the end of Preston Park to the Southern extreme of the end of the pier! There are also a few notable additions outside of this patch.

The total number of pubs and bars covered by this edition is 300 but there might be a couple of others hidden away – drop us a line if you know of one!

The System

The aim is to provide a fair, balanced and objective assessment of every pub in the city using a standard system so that bars that appear remarkably different in themselves can be compared on a level playing field.

Pub jurors are the key to the system – the more the merrier! They pay unannounced rating visits to pubs and score the unsuspecting hostelry against six different factors.

At the time of going to press there are seven pub jurors spanning a twenty year age range and including a CAMRA member, a cider drinker, a rocker and one woman! This eclectic mix generates a remarkably balanced scoring system. Six of these are Brighton residents, with one living in a nearby village. All of them have lived in the area for at least ten years.

So what are the factors to rate a pub against? Well…..

1. **Atmosphere**

This is actually the hardest factor to define. It describes that quality about a place that makes you feel happy there. It might be that it's kicking or that it's a good place to go with a group of friends. It could be the other people there, or the lack of them. It's the feel of a pub rather than anything concrete. Mostly these pubs will be comfortably full with a good crowd of people who are enjoying themselves.

2. **Barstaff**

Good barstaff are quick to serve the right person with the right drink for the right price. They will chat to you or leave you alone – as you like. They'll go out of their way to make your drinking experience a pleasant one.

3. **Beer**

This is not just beer, but all drinks. To get a good score a pub will serve a good range of high quality drinks for reasonable prices. Obviously there is a heavy focus on beer here, so expect a pub that just serves expensive bottled lager to fare poorly.

4. **Décor/Garden**

This is about how a place looks and how comfortable it is. Sunny, well-tended beer gardens, nice art or well-stocked wooden bookcases are a good way to score well, while worn carpets with plastic chairs will have jurors headed for the door.

5. **Entertainment**

Encompassing a wide range of diversions from live music, DJs and quizzes through pool, darts, pinball round to newspapers, boardgames and machines. Some Brighton pubs even have cabaret, cinema or saunas!

6. **Food**

Obviously this covers the quality of food that a pub serves, with range and price also important elements of the score.

Jurors rank the factors in order of importance to them. The combination of all the jurors' rankings is used to create a weighting for each factor. These weightings are used to combine the individual scores to create the overall rating for each pub. At the moment by far the most important ratings are, predictably, Atmosphere and Beer. Food is the least important factor in the overall pub rating.

Each juror scores each pub they visit from 0-4 on each factor. All the jurors' scores are then averaged to produce a reliable group assessment for each pub.

So you fancy becoming a pub juror? Well it's tougher than you'd expect. Many wannabe jurors have fallen at the first hurdle of actually submitting scores – a rather crucial exercise! If you do get into the scoring habit then you are required to score 50 pubs before your scores will be merged into the ratings system. This is to ensure that the overall scores are not distorted by the addition of just someone's favourite drinking holes and that the juror has a wide range of pubs to assess their scores against. On top of all this, think of the commitment that is required with 300 pubs to share your time between – that's over a pub every night for a year, with weekends off. It's a tough job, but someone's gotta do it!

The Results

Well, you can safely say that we haven't been soft in our reviewing. Only three pubs in the town receive scores over 90%! The average of all the pubs is 59% and 78 pubs are given an overall score below 50%. Sorry to all those places, but it's all your own fault!

Cheers!

Juror Portraits

No names, no pack drill, but here is a quick run down of the current Brighton pub jurors:

Mr. H
The most senior juror in terms of number of pubs visited as well as in age, Mr. H enjoys a quality pint of bitter in a quality establishment. No plastic plants for this fellow! His favourite pub is the Basketmakers, closely followed by the Hop Poles, Prestonville Arms and Blind Busker.

Mr. A
With favourites of the Sidewinder, Battle of Trafalgar and the Basketmakers, Mr. A prizes objectivity over personal favourites in his marking. He'll drink lager, bitter, stout or cocktails – basically anything in a glass. His preferred place of drinking has to have a bit of life.

Mr. B
A fairly new father of one, Mr. B has had his drinking sessions curtailed by nappy changing, but in his day his preferred pub valued atmosphere and entertainment over beer. He's a lager drinking, football watching, gambling executive with a taste for a hot curry. Personal favourites: the Basketmakers, Regency and the Cricketers.

Mr. E
An occasionally dangerous professional cider-drinker, Mr. E still feels like a student and favours the younger atmosphere for his alcohol consumption. Favourite hang-outs are the Hop Poles, Ali-Cats and Sidewinder. On weeknights Mr. E likes to frequent pub quizzes and is expert at coming 3rd.

Mr. T
Another young father, but this time of two, Mr. T is the only juror not resident in Brighton, hiding out in Plumpton and making regular forays into the big city purely for the sake of research. An ardent Seagulls fan, Mr. T also likes a good pint of bitter to wash away his sorrows and favours modern pubs of quality like the Hop Poles, Basketmakers and Open House.

Miss C
Currently the only woman on the team, Miss C has her work cut out objectively representing the views of the entire fairer sex. She is the only juror who rates Beer as low as being the 4th most important facet of a pub. Her premier haunts are the Shakespeare's Head, Pub With No Name and the Park Crescent.

Mr. M
Band member and full time artist and rocker, Mr. M knows what he wants from a pub and it is Atmosphere, Beer and Entertainment in that order. It tells you a lot about him that his top drinking dens are the Hobgoblin, Ali-Cats and the Free Butt. Lager and loud music make him a happy man.

THE VERDICT

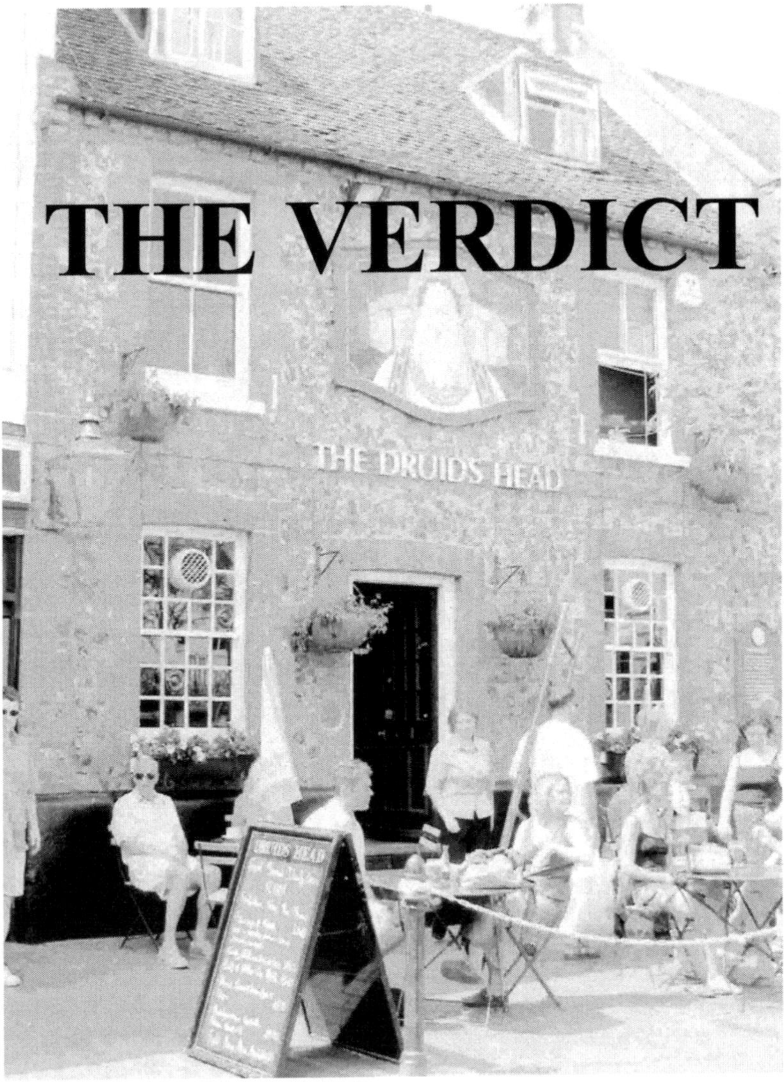

Brighton's Best Pubs: The Verdict

Brighton's Best Pubs: The Top Ten

For the impatient amongst you, here is a list of the ten best pubs in Brighton with their overall rating.

1. Basketmakers, 94%

This is the long-standing highest scoring pub of the Brighton pub jurors and that is backed up by the fact that it is usually packed to the gunnels. It is friendly, with good food, beer and weird wines. No machines. The décor is interesting and previous drinkers have left messages in the antique tobacco tin collection on the walls.

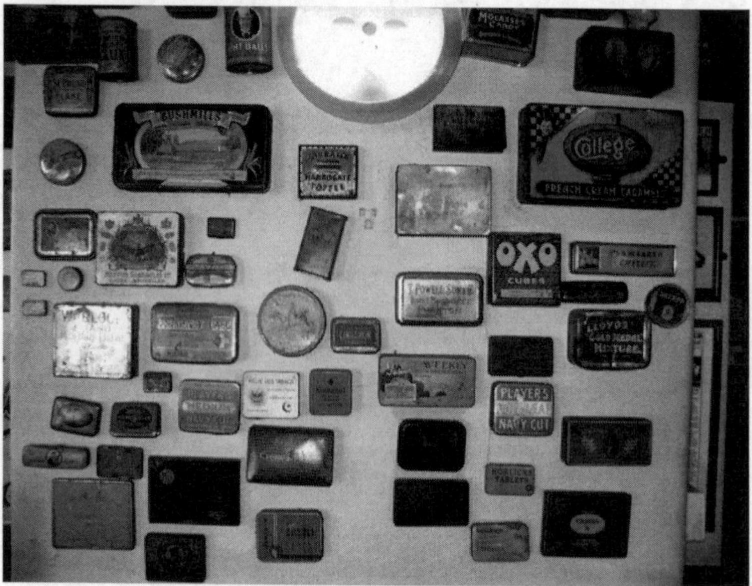

The Basketmakers' tobacco tins

2. Open House, 90%

This is a fairly new Zel-run pub/bar (only a couple of years old). It has very arty decor and customers, in keeping with the thespian ambience of this part of Brighton. It features good service, food, varied entertainment and a very large courtyard-come-beer garden, which is fantastic in the summer.

3. The Hop Poles, 90%

Relaxed, modern pub with good beer, great food, music, garden, jars of sweets, friendly barstaff, modern art (hub-cap octopus on the roof and crocodile on the outside wall) and chilled music. Why aren't all modern pubs like this? Can often be just too full.

4. The Pub With No Name, 87%

This no-name pub is a warm, interesting, locals' pub like a house party with lots of rooms & friendly barstaff. It's well worth the climb up Southover Street. Good food, which you can usually see lots of people eating!

5. The Dragon, 85%

This is a hidden gem of a pub at the far end of Kemptown has amazing décor and an interesting group of punters. There is a great and varied food menu.

6. Sidewinder, 84%

You can spot this one by the disturbing crab/eye painting on the outside. This medium sized bar is always packed and no wonder given the great music, comfy seats and modern art decor. A good selection of beers on draught, a large beer garden and some interesting games round it off nicely.

7. Regency, 84%

Another hard-to-find pub, it has possibly the most outrageous and ostentatious decor of any pub in Brighton. There is an interesting mix of punters and barstaff. Definitely gay-friendly, very camp and it features amazing disco toilets.

8. Prestonville Arms, 84%

This is the sister pub to the Basketmakers, but hidden away in the back streets behind the station. It's got the same quality Gales beer, great food and good regular quiz. Very comfortable, with a small beer garden. It's a bit of a boozers' pub, due to the beer quality and location.

9. Walmer, 83%

This pub features wild colours, fish tanks and a popular regular pub quiz. Good local colour and friendly atmosphere make you glad you made the journey. A massive selection of music and friendly barstaff add nicely to the mix.

10. The Wellington, 82%

A traditional, busy Kemptown pub, the "Wellie" (so-called) has efficient barstaff, reasonable beer and a friendly atmosphere. Fairly spacious - you should be able to find a table if you want one. Raises lots of money for charity.

The Different Areas of Brighton

This section is for the lazy amongst you. It breaks down Brighton into twelve geographical areas and tells you the best pub in each area.

The Brighton Seafront

This is likely to be an early stop for most first-time visitors to Brighton, especially in the summer, when the pebbled beach is hard to resist. In fact Brighton beach was recently voted the 20th best beach in the world! The 'arches' area between the road and the beach has been massively renovated in recent years and is a joy to stroll along, with cafes, bars, restaurants, shops and rather strangely, a gym. Obviously there is the Brighton pier, which has three bars on it, currently the only pier you can go on following the collapse and fire on the West pier,. Then there are a stunning nine bars along the beach between the two piers. Five more pubs/bars along the road make up most of the 21 drinking establishments in this area. The ideal environment boosts the scores of most of the so-so bars and there is no truly bad place – after all, you can always drink on the beach!
The "Fortunes of War" easily stands out as the best place, with a rating of 74%.

The Clock Tower

This area covers the pubs around Churchill Square shopping area and the full-on nightlife area of West Street. This is possibly the worst street for pubs in Brighton and is definitely so on a Friday or Saturday night. This area is to be avoided by anyone with any sense who is over the age of 25. This general advice is reinforced by the poor ratings of the pubs – for the 14 pubs in this Area, the average rating is 51%, the lowest score of any of the sections of the town.

Walkabout gets the highest rating at 69%, the best of a bad bunch, the fact that a chain pub wins shows the competition isn't up to much.

The Lanes

This area used to be the old village of Brighthelmstone back before the Prince Regent started to make Brighton fashionable. The boundaries of it are clearly marked by North, East and West Streets (South Street is buried beneath the beach). This small area has a stunning 35 pubs packed into it, and probably about a hundred jewellery shops! Weekends see stag and hen parties making their way between many of these places before the survivors drag themselves to a nightclub or the beach. The average rating of this mass of pubs is a quite respectable 59%, but there are definitely a few dogs in this area to steer clear of…

The fabulous Hop Poles is the top pub, with 90%, but the very different Ali Cats is also here with 82%.

North Laine

Commonly known as "The North Lanes", this small, laid-back area of town features lots of alternative shops and a variety of other distractions, such as street markets and the stunning Brighton Pavillion. You will walk along the edge of the North Laine if you walk out of the station and down Queen's Road towards the sea. There are 36 pubs tucked away in these streets, with usually a pub on every one, and a solid 59% average for the lot.

The Weird and Wonderful Brighton Pavillion

The area also contains the best pub in Brighton, the very traditional Basketmaker's Arms, but if that isn't to your taste, you could give the dark, rockin' Hobgoblin a try, which with an 81% rating is not to be dismissed lightly.

Western Road

This is a large area, encompassing everything West of Churchill Square, up to the border with Hove. You'll get into this area by walking along either Western Road itself or along the seafront. There is a maze of streets here and some of the 36 pubs in this area could prove pretty difficult to find!

The unique Regency is the top pub in the Area with a strong 84% rating, comparing very well with the average score of 61%. This average comprises a lot of awful pubs, but also includes several very good ones.

Seven Dials

This area is centred on a roundabout North West of the station, but also includes a lot of pubs in the Area around the station to the West of Queens Road. With an average score of 64% for its seventeen pubs, this is Area has statistically the best group of pubs in the city. This isn't really surprising considering that four pubs score near the 80% mark and only one scores lower than 40%.

Best pub in the Area by a whisker is the Gales pub, The Prestonville Arms (84%) which is the sister pub of the Basketmakers. Great beer, food and décor, but it isn't that exciting in there, so you could go into any of the Caxton Arms (81%), Shakespeare's Head (80%), or the Battle of Trafalgar (79%).

St. James' Street

This is the fastest growing district for bars in town, with little places popping up all the time in this cosmopolitan area. It comprises the roads to the East of the pier and the Steine, and with eleven of its 30 pubs/bars being gay-orientated it is THE place to go if you are that way inclined. In fact, by the latest reckoning, this Area of Brighton contains half of all the gay bars in town, including a couple of lesbian joints. Don't worry, most of the places are not full on "police academy" style gay bars, although a couple are……

The Sidewinder, with 84%, is the top bar in this section of town, with the rest of pubs evenly ranging from very good to very bad indeed. The surprisingly low 57% average for the area is the fourth lowest in town, probably because of the three dire places with a score below 40%.

Ditchling Road Area

Heading out of town on the London Road takes you to a big junction called Preston Circus, recognisable by the fire station and Duke of York's independent cinema (which is always showing interesting films) with its stripey legs in the air. A fairly wide area around this junction contains 24 drinking holes, some of which truly are holes rather than any other term. Ditchling Road neatly bisects the area, which spans across to the Lewes road on its western edge.

The arty, Zel-chain bar The Open House is easily the best of the bunch at 90%, though you'll have to walk up a considerable hill to find it on an unlikely sidestreet. Only nine of the other places in this area score over 60%, and with it being the second worst area for pubs there is little motivation to plan a pub crawl here. Instead, we've done it for you, though it does not come highly recommended.

The Preston Circus area is also famed for containing the currently worst scoring pub in town, but you'll have to find out which that one is for yourselves....

Hanover

For the purposes of this book the Hanover district also includes the pubs on the Eastern side of the Lewes Road, over to Freshfield Road on the West. Hanover is a reasonably fashionable part of town to the North East of the centre, where the cool but relaxed like to hang out and live. It is mainly made up of the streets going up serious hills from the Lewes Road, the main ones you'll find pubs on being Elm Grove, Islingword Road and Southover Street.

The coolness of the district transfers to the quality of the pubs, with its 30 pubs scoring an average of 62% - taking the 2nd spot for the best section of town. The top establishments of the area are the Pub With No Name (87%) and the Walmer Castle (83%), both very similar and popular chill-out joints. In addition a horde of quality Local pubs score in the high sixties and seventies.

The Edges Of Town

The final three zones of Brighton make up the Eastern, Western and Northern edges of the city. In some ways they are not really edges at all – on the West Hove continues into Portslade and on the East Kemptown fades into suburbs.

The Eastern 'Edge': Kemptown

It is hard to say where East Brighton ends and Kemptown begins, but we've gone with the end of St. James' Street as being the start of Kemptown proper. Although often thought of as gay, this grouping of 22 bars contains only one gay pub. We've chosen to include the Brighton Marina's five bars in this section, too.

The pubs score a reasonable average of 59% with the best by far being the Dragon, Wellington and Rock Inn, all coming in with stunning 80%+ ratings. Lots of the other pubs merit a look though, most of them having a friendly and relaxed atmosphere, and there is something distinctive about most of them.

The Western 'Edge': Hove

"Do you live in Brighton?" "No, Hove, actually." As the old local jokey saying goes, with Hove-ites allegedly looking down on their rather low-budget neighbours. This doesn't really hold for pubs, though, with a large number of the 25 pubs and bars in Hove being smokier and grottier than their now groovier sister-town. This doesn't seem to have put off a seemingly never-ending convoy of celebrities buying up houses in Hove though!

This guide covers the Hove area up to a Western border of Sackville Road, which means that it does not cover any of Portslade's pubs, with the exception of the rather special Portland Rock Bar, which scores 78% mainly due to its excellent live music.

The Exchange (72%) marginally triumphs as the second best pub in the area, though there are a number of pleasant places to while away the hours in the company of a pint glass. Hove's average score is 60%, just over the overall average for the City as a whole.

The Northern 'Edge': North Brighton

Not really an edge at all, this section captures all the pubs not covered so far that are in the more Northerly section of town, plus a few notable pubs on the outskirts of Brighton which merit inclusion.

There are a small number of pubs in Brighton's suburbs that have been excluded. This guide covers everywhere that anyone but a local to these pubs is likely to go and all the major pubs on the roads into town, including the landmark Black Lion in Patcham.

Two pubs on either side of Preston Park, The Park View (76%) and The Preston Park Tavern (71%) stand out as being the top places to quaff in this grouping. While not the worst in this lot with a 45% rating, the Devil's Dyke Tavern is probably the one most deserving a warning to the public as a very poor establishment in a very beautiful location. The average for this small group of twelve is 58%.

Best Speciality Pubs

Here we'll cover the pubs that score well in each category. Just where would you go for a good pint? Where for a good meal? Where when you need to be entertained? When you're on your own, where are the best barstaff to chat to? Where to stare at the pretty walls or where has the best atmosphere?

The Top Five Drinking Dens

1. Basketmakers Arms
2. Evening Star
3. Cliftonville Inn
4. Prestonville Arms
5. Blind Busker

No surprise to see the Basketmakers at the top of the list again. The 100% Beer rating that the jurors have unanimously given the pub goes a long way to making it the overall top pub in town. Great Gales beers, Becks on draught, a serious selection of whiskies and a wide selection of fruit wine go a long way to justifying this score. Its Gales sister pub the Prestonville is not shy of the mark either.

The Basketmaker's whisky selection!

The Evening Star is there purely on beer. Really it has to be seen to be experienced and is the favourite haunt of a good many CAMRA members.

The Cliftonville is a Wetherspoons, with a fantastic choice of real ales at low, low prices. It's a shame about the feel of the place. The Blind Busker really seems to make an effort on beer, with a wide choice on draught and a load of specialist Belgian beers available in bottles.

The Top Five Places to Feel the Vibe

1. Open House
2. Basketmakers Arms
3. Hop Poles
4. Ali Cats
5. Pub With No Name

These are the places that the jurors have given top marks to for Atmosphere. Looking at the five, each of them seems to have a distinct quality that makes it such a great place to be. The Open House tops the list, cool and modern with an ever-changing selection of art covering the walls and a happy buzz of conversation about the place. The Pub With No Name is more like a house party than a pub – relaxed and welcoming with few pretentions. There's the Basketmakers again, just a great place to sup on a pint. The Hop Poles is different again, with a youthful clientele and a feeling that anything could happen. Finally the Ali Cats is a packed dive of lively drinkers who can either be starting the build up to a clubbing session or in the midst of a long day's quaffing.

The Open House garden is very chilled out

The Top Five Pubs for Grub

1. Basketmakers
2. Dragon
3. Sanctuary Café
4. More
5. Hop Poles

These five win the battle for the places to eat whilst you drink. The Basketmakers simply serves up top quality pub grub. The Dragon and Hop Poles offer modern fusion food, ensuring that you can't fail to find something that you want to munch on and you will be pleasantly surprised with your choice rather than disappointed! More at certain times of the day is almost more of a restaurant than a bar and similarly the Sanctuary Café can be more of a café than a pub – though live bands on some evenings define the difference. Perhaps worthy of a honourable mention is The George, which won the "National Vegetarian Food Pub of the Year" for 2002, though recent reports are that the food has gone downhill somewhat.

The Top Five Places to be Entertained

1. Portland Rock Bar
2. Walkabout
3. Bombay Bar
4. Free Butt
5. Ali Cats

The Portland Rock Bar tops the list on the basis of its fantastic live music. Walkabout comes second due to the masses of TV screens, special events and games available. Bombay Bar is no doubt second just on the basis of its live (jazz) music - though rumours exist of other entertainments - as is the Free Butt. Ali Cats serves up a selection of novelty entertainment in the shape of a bowling alley, films on a big screen and the atmosphere of the place itself! The Smuggler Arms in 6th just misses out but could be there purely on the entertainment value of the other drinkers after 9pm, but probably features due to the pool tables, bar billiards and quiz/fruit machines. That's without even mentioning the eclectic décor!

Ali Cats has its own cinema!

The Top Five for Service

1. Chez Nous
2. "14"
3. The Hanover
4. Le Lion D'Or
5. No Name Bar

These are the top pubs for "Barstaff" and this ranges from the sheer quality of service provided in "14", to the chat and flexibility of the bar staff at Chez Nous. Le Lion D'Or, No Name Bar and Hanover have consistently friendly, helpful and efficient barstaff and are justly recognised on this list for that.

The Top Five for Looks

1. The Boardwalk
2. Hop Poles
3. Ebony Room
4. Le Lion D'Or
5. Tzar Bar

The Boardwalk is the nearest pub the Palace Pier and its beach views, courtyard and stylish interior are hard to beat for a score against "Décor/Garden". The Hop Poles is small but perfectly formed with a pleasant walled garden and interesting hub-cap animal sculptures. Le Lion D'Or and Ebony Rooms are simply swish and stylish. The Tzar Bar has its industrial-style indoors and large beach-based posing area to lift it into this section.

The Boardwalk 'garden' is the beach

The Top Five for Totty (Straight)

1. Fishbowl
2. Smugglers
3. West Quay
4. Tzar Bar
5. The Standard

The "Totty" rating was done for a bit of a laugh and actually does not contribute the overall rating of our pubs. It reflects the quality and quantity of (seemingly) available totty in the pubs, both male and female.
There's an interesting selection here for the very subjective rating of places to go for (straight) totty. The Fishbowl and Smugglers are good any night for a mix of potentially friendly singles and masses of hen and stag groups. West Quay is no doubt the place of choice for the sexy Marina set, whilst the skimpily dressed single beach lovers hang out at the Tzar Bar. The bar-come-club The Standard is no doubt here on the basis of its packed late-night dancing and drinking status.

The Top Five for Totty (Gay)

1. Amsterdam
2. Dr. Brighton's
3. Bulldog
4. Regency
5. Queen's Head (Steine)

The talent checks you out as soon as you walk in the door at the Amsterdam, whereas Dr. Brighton's crowd is a more relaxed and friendly one. The Bulldog is VERY gay and a good place to pick up a Village People look-a-like, in contrast to the elegantly golden Regency where you will be in good company camping it up. In the Queens' Head the stage show is the ideal means of breaking the ice as you get to know someone new or old……

THE A-Z

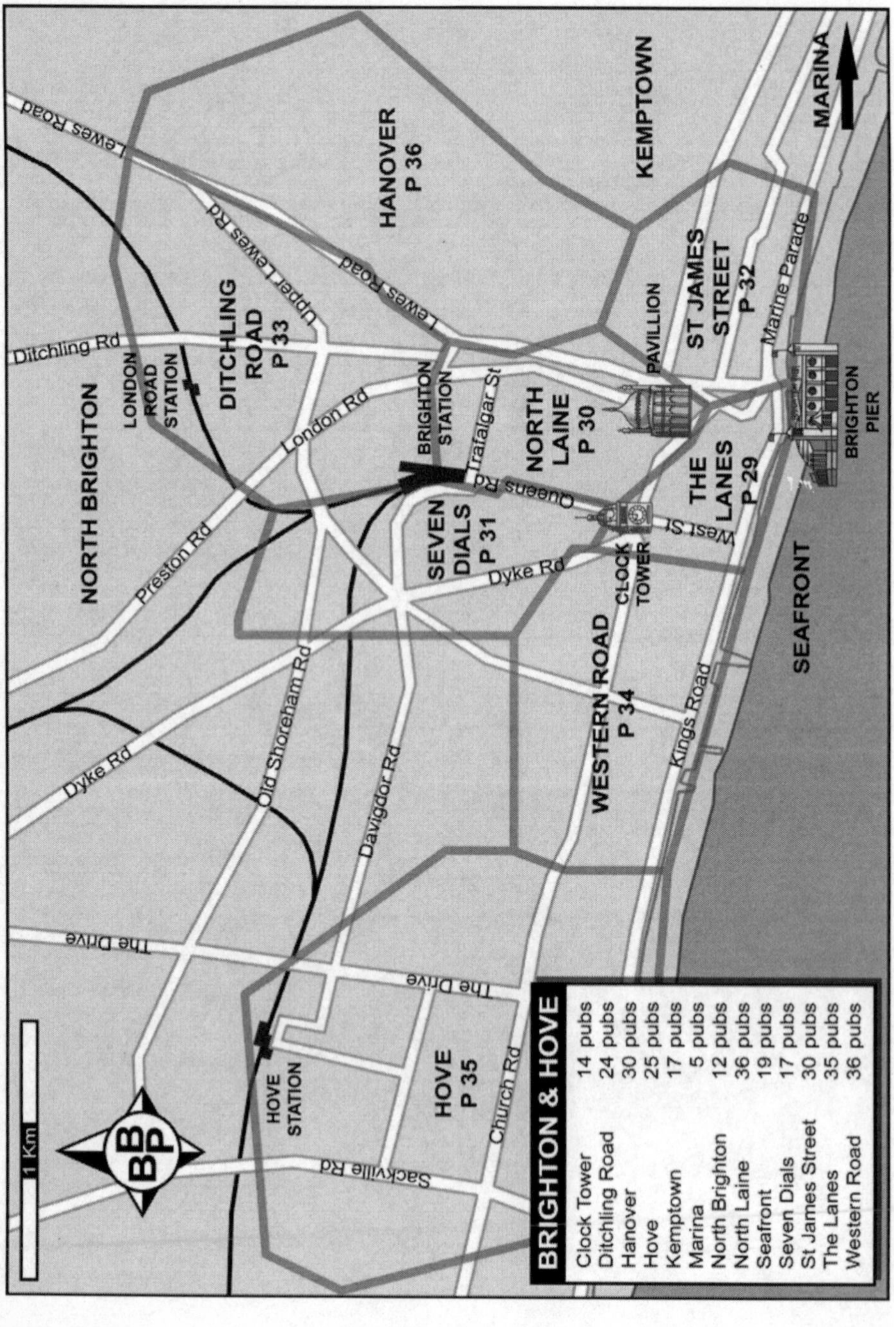
BRIGHTON & HOVE
Clock Tower 14 pubs
Ditchling Road 24 pubs
Hanover 30 pubs
Hove 25 pubs
Kemptown 17 pubs
Marina 5 pubs
North Brighton 12 pubs
North Laine 36 pubs
Seafront 19 pubs
Seven Dials 17 pubs
St James Street 30 pubs
The Lanes 35 pubs
Western Road 36 pubs
1 Km
NORTH BRIGHTON
LONDON ROAD STATION
DITCHLING ROAD P 33
HANOVER P 36
KEMPTOWN
MARINA
ST JAMES STREET P 32
PAVILLION
NORTH LAINE P 30
BRIGHTON STATION
SEVEN DIALS P 31
THE LANES P 29
CLOCK TOWER
WESTERN ROAD P 34
SEAFRONT
BRIGHTON PIER
HOVE P 35
HOVE STATION
Lewes Road
Upper Lewes Rd
Ditchling Rd
London Rd
Preston Rd
Trafalgar St
Queens Rd
West St
Dyke Rd
Marine Parade
Kings Road
Old Shoreham Rd
Davigdor Rd
The Drive
Church Rd
Sackville Rd

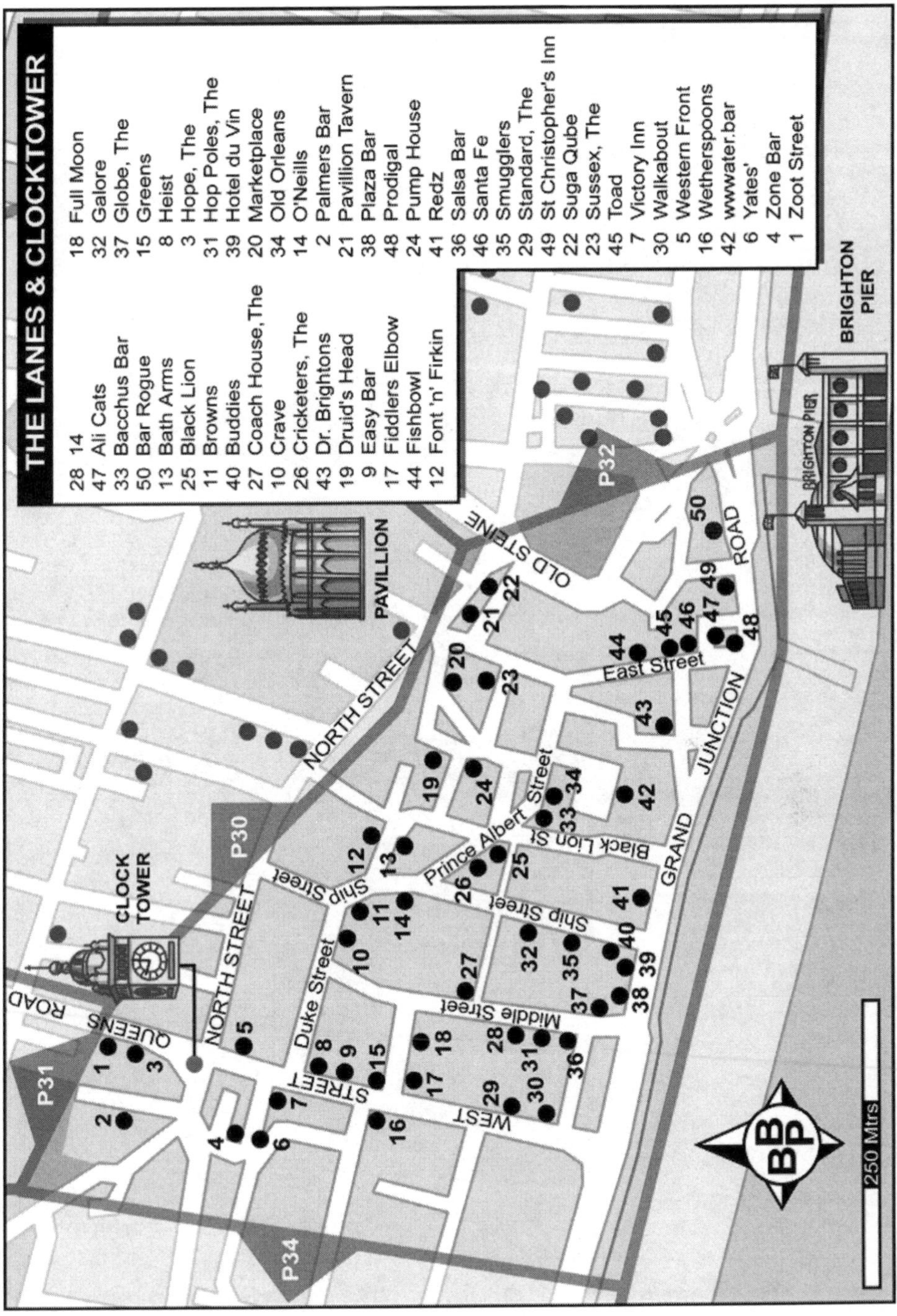
THE LANES & CLOCKTOWER
28 14
47 Ali Cats
33 Bacchus Bar
50 Bar Rogue
13 Bath Arms
25 Black Lion
11 Browns
40 Buddies
27 Coach House, The
10 Crave
26 Cricketers, The
43 Dr. Brightons
19 Druid's Head
9 Easy Bar
17 Fiddlers Elbow
44 Fishbowl
12 Font 'n' Firkin
18 Full Moon
32 Galore
37 Globe, The
15 Greens
8 Heist
3 Hope, The
31 Hop Poles, The
39 Hotel du Vin
20 Marketplace
34 Old Orleans
14 O'Neills
2 Palmers Bar
21 Pavillion Tavern
38 Plaza Bar
48 Prodigal
24 Pump House
41 Redz
36 Salsa Bar
46 Santa Fe
35 Smugglers
29 Standard, The
49 St Christopher's Inn
22 Suga Qube
23 Sussex, The
45 Toad
7 Victory Inn
30 Walkabout
5 Western Front
16 Wetherspoons
42 wwwater.bar
6 Yates'
4 Zone Bar
1 Zoot Street
CLOCK TOWER
PAVILLION
BRIGHTON PIER
BRIGHTON PIER
QUEENS ROAD
NORTH STREET
NORTH STREET
WEST STREET
Duke Street
Middle Street
Ship Street
Ship Street
Prince Albert Street
Black Lion St
East Street
OLD STEINE
GRAND JUNCTION ROAD
P30
P31
P32
P34
250 Mtrs

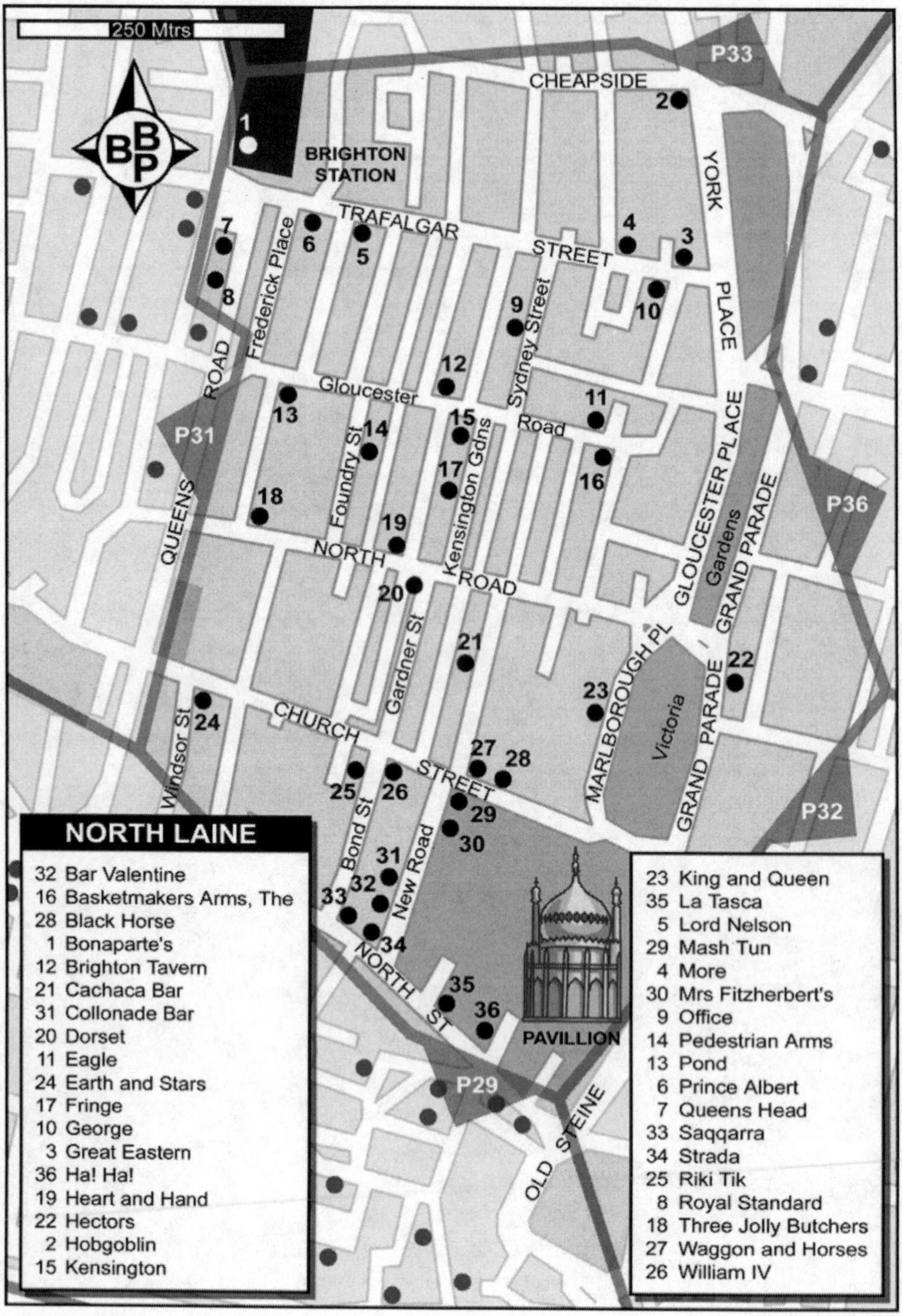
250 Mtrs
BRIGHTON STATION
CHEAPSIDE
TRAFALGAR STREET
YORK PLACE
QUEENS ROAD
Frederick Place
Sydney Street
Gloucester Road
Foundry St
Kensington Gdns
NORTH ROAD
GLOUCESTER PLACE
Gardens
GRAND PARADE
Gardner St
MARLBOROUGH PL
Victoria
Windsor St
CHURCH STREET
Bond St
New Road
NORTH ST
OLD STEINE
PAVILLION
P29
P31
P32
P33
P36
NORTH LAINE
32 Bar Valentine
16 Basketmakers Arms, The
28 Black Horse
1 Bonaparte's
12 Brighton Tavern
21 Cachaca Bar
31 Collonade Bar
20 Dorset
11 Eagle
24 Earth and Stars
17 Fringe
10 George
3 Great Eastern
36 Ha! Ha!
19 Heart and Hand
22 Hectors
2 Hobgoblin
15 Kensington
23 King and Queen
35 La Tasca
5 Lord Nelson
29 Mash Tun
4 More
30 Mrs Fitzherbert's
9 Office
14 Pedestrian Arms
13 Pond
6 Prince Albert
7 Queens Head
33 Saqqarra
34 Strada
25 Riki Tik
8 Royal Standard
18 Three Jolly Butchers
27 Waggon and Horses
26 William IV

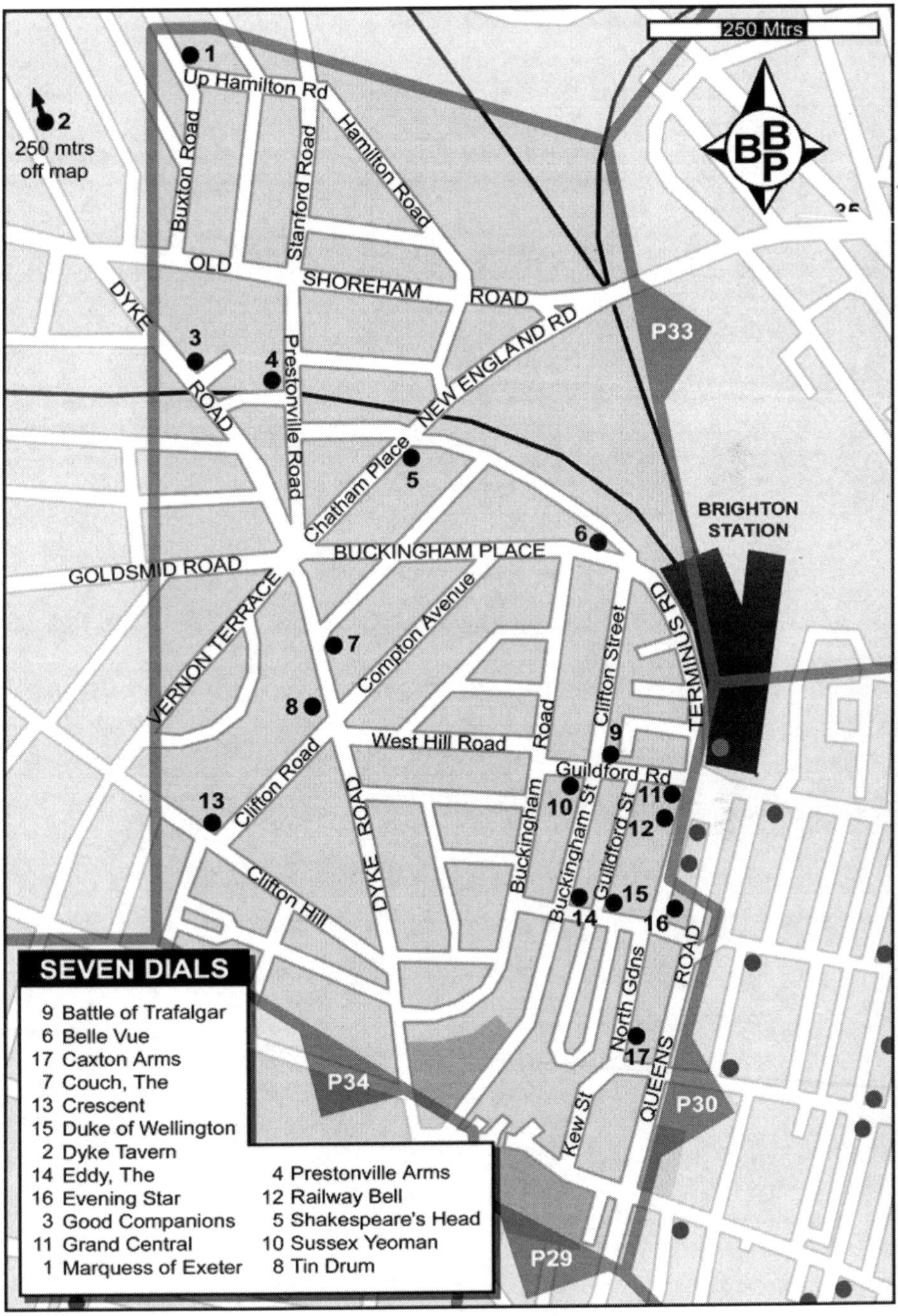
250 Mtrs
2
250 mtrs off map
Up Hamilton Rd
Buxton Road
Stanford Road
Hamilton Road
OLD SHOREHAM ROAD
DYKE ROAD
Prestonville Road
NEW ENGLAND RD
Chatham Place
P33
BRIGHTON STATION
BUCKINGHAM PLACE
GOLDSMID ROAD
VERNON TERRACE
Compton Avenue
Clifton Street
TERMINUS RD
West Hill Road
Guildford Rd
Clifton Road
DYKE ROAD
Buckingham Road
Buckingham St
Guildford St
Clifton Hill
North Gdns
QUEENS ROAD
Kew St
P34
P30
P29
SEVEN DIALS
9 Battle of Trafalgar
6 Belle Vue
17 Caxton Arms
7 Couch, The
13 Crescent
15 Duke of Wellington
2 Dyke Tavern
14 Eddy, The
16 Evening Star
3 Good Companions
11 Grand Central
1 Marquess of Exeter
4 Prestonville Arms
12 Railway Bell
5 Shakespeare's Head
10 Sussex Yeoman
8 Tin Drum

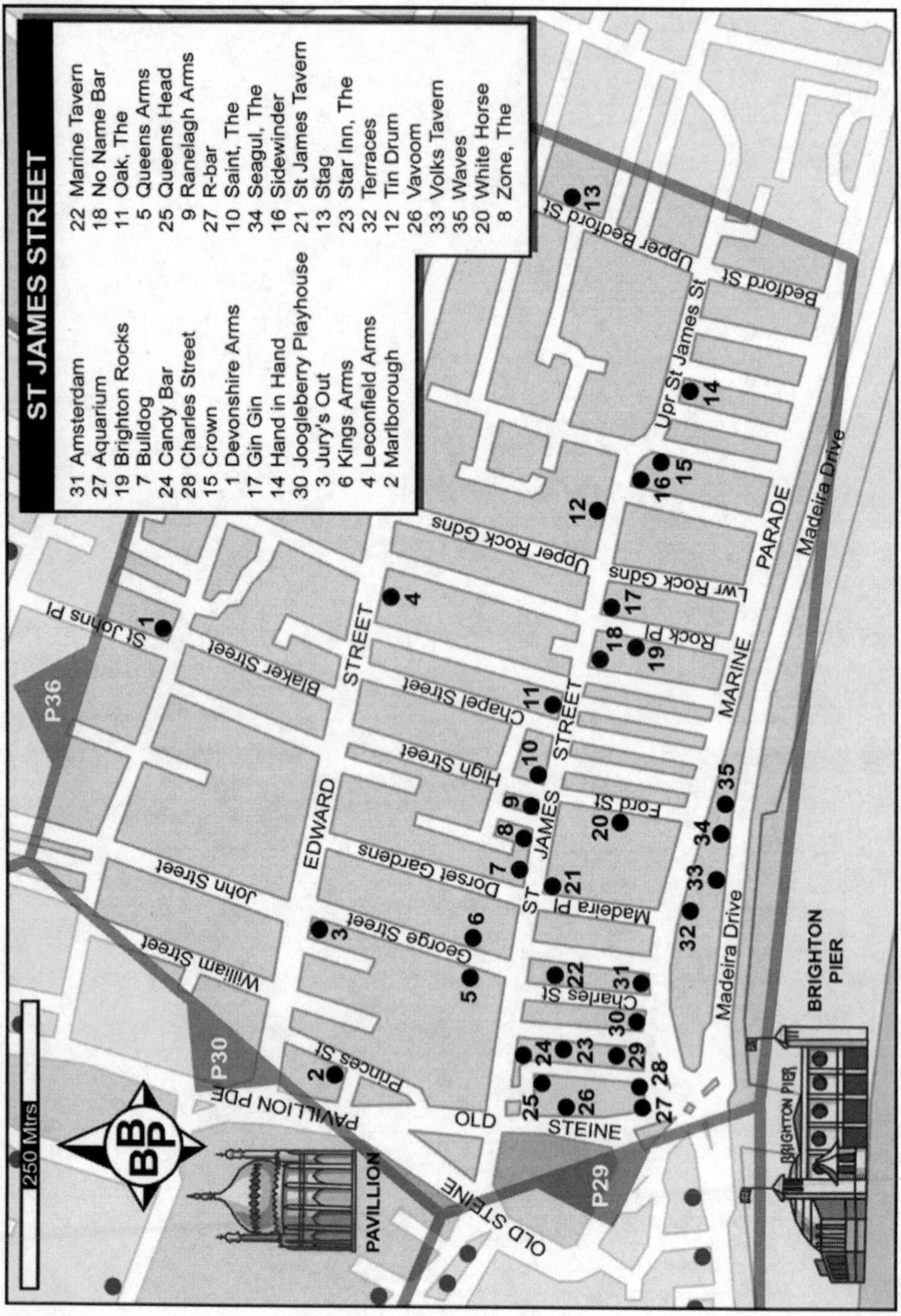
ST JAMES STREET
31 Amsterdam
27 Aquarium
19 Brighton Rocks
7 Bulldog
24 Candy Bar
28 Charles Street
15 Crown
1 Devonshire Arms
17 Gin Gin
14 Hand in Hand
30 Joogleberry Playhouse
3 Jury's Out
6 Kings Arms
4 Leconfield Arms
2 Marlborough
22 Marine Tavern
18 No Name Bar
11 Oak, The
5 Queens Arms
25 Queens Head
9 Ranelagh Arms
27 R-bar
10 Saint, The
34 Seagul, The
16 Sidewinder
21 St James Tavern
13 Stag
23 Star Inn, The
32 Terraces
12 Tin Drum
26 Vavoom
33 Volks Tavern
35 Waves
20 White Horse
8 Zone, The
250 Mtrs
PAVILLION
PAVILLION PDE
OLD STEINE
OLD STEINE
Princes St
William Street
John Street
George Street
Dorset Gardens
EDWARD STREET
Blaker Street
St Johns Pl
High Street
Chapel Street
ST JAMES STREET
Charles St
Madeira Pl
Ford St
Rock Pl
Lwr Rock Gdns
Upper Rock Gdns
Upr St James St
Upper Bedford St
Bedford St
MARINE PARADE
Madeira Drive
Madeira Drive
BRIGHTON PIER
BRIGHTON PIER
P29
P30
P36

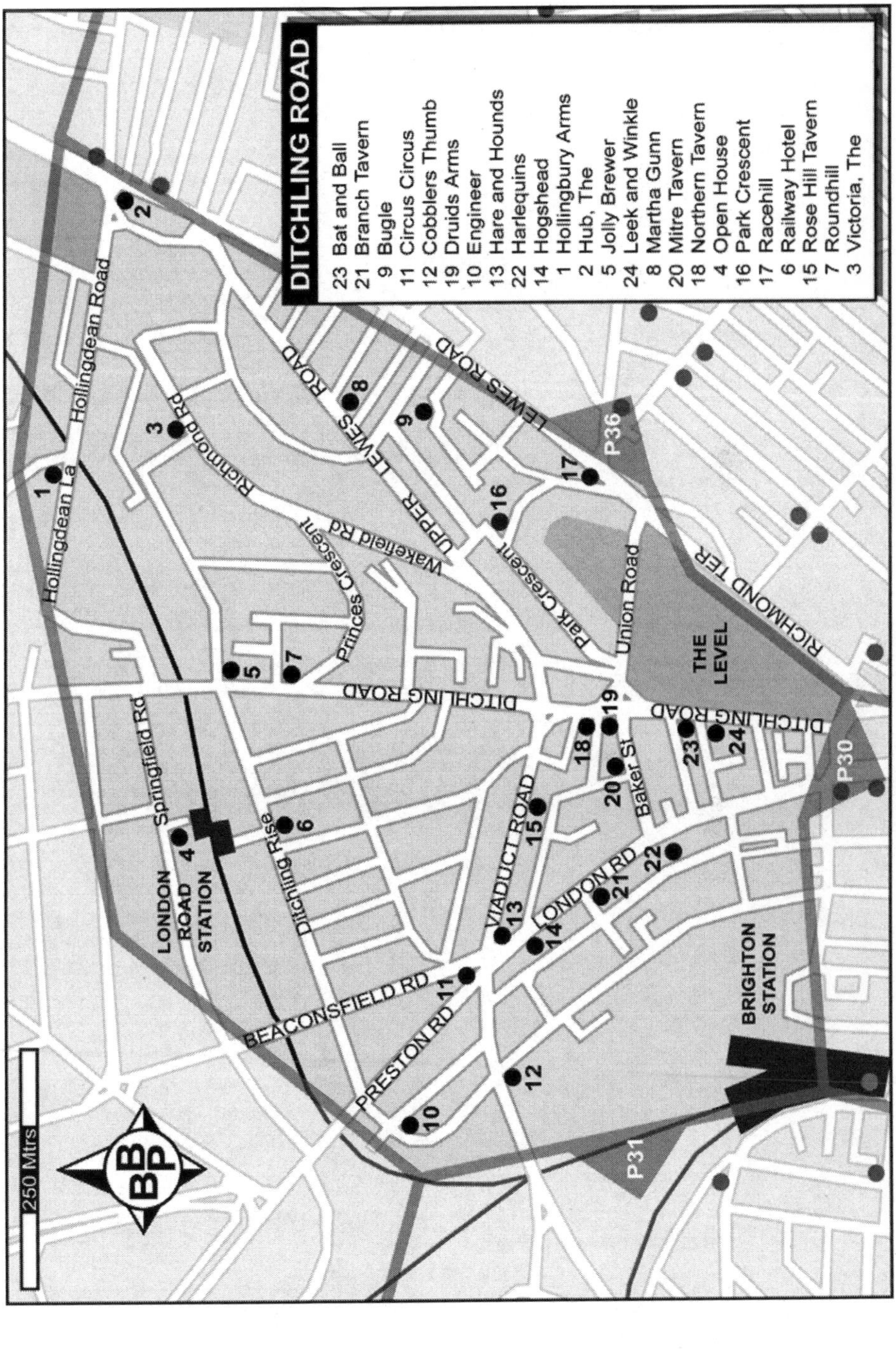
DITCHLING ROAD
23 Bat and Ball
21 Branch Tavern
9 Bugle
11 Circus Circus
12 Cobblers Thumb
19 Druids Arms
10 Engineer
13 Hare and Hounds
22 Harlequins
14 Hogshead
1 Hollingbury Arms
2 Hub, The
5 Jolly Brewer
24 Leek and Winkle
8 Martha Gunn
20 Mitre Tavern
18 Northern Tavern
4 Open House
16 Park Crescent
17 Racehill
6 Railway Hotel
15 Rose Hill Tavern
7 Roundhill
3 Victoria, The
250 Mtrs
Hollingdean Road
Hollingdean La
Richmond Rd
LEWES ROAD
UPPER LEWES ROAD
Wakefield Rd
Princes Crescent
Park Crescent
Union Road
RICHMOND TER
THE LEVEL
DITCHLING ROAD
Springfield Rd
LONDON ROAD STATION
Ditchling Rise
VIADUCT ROAD
Baker St
LONDON RD
BEACONSFIELD RD
PRESTON RD
BRIGHTON STATION
P36
P30
P31

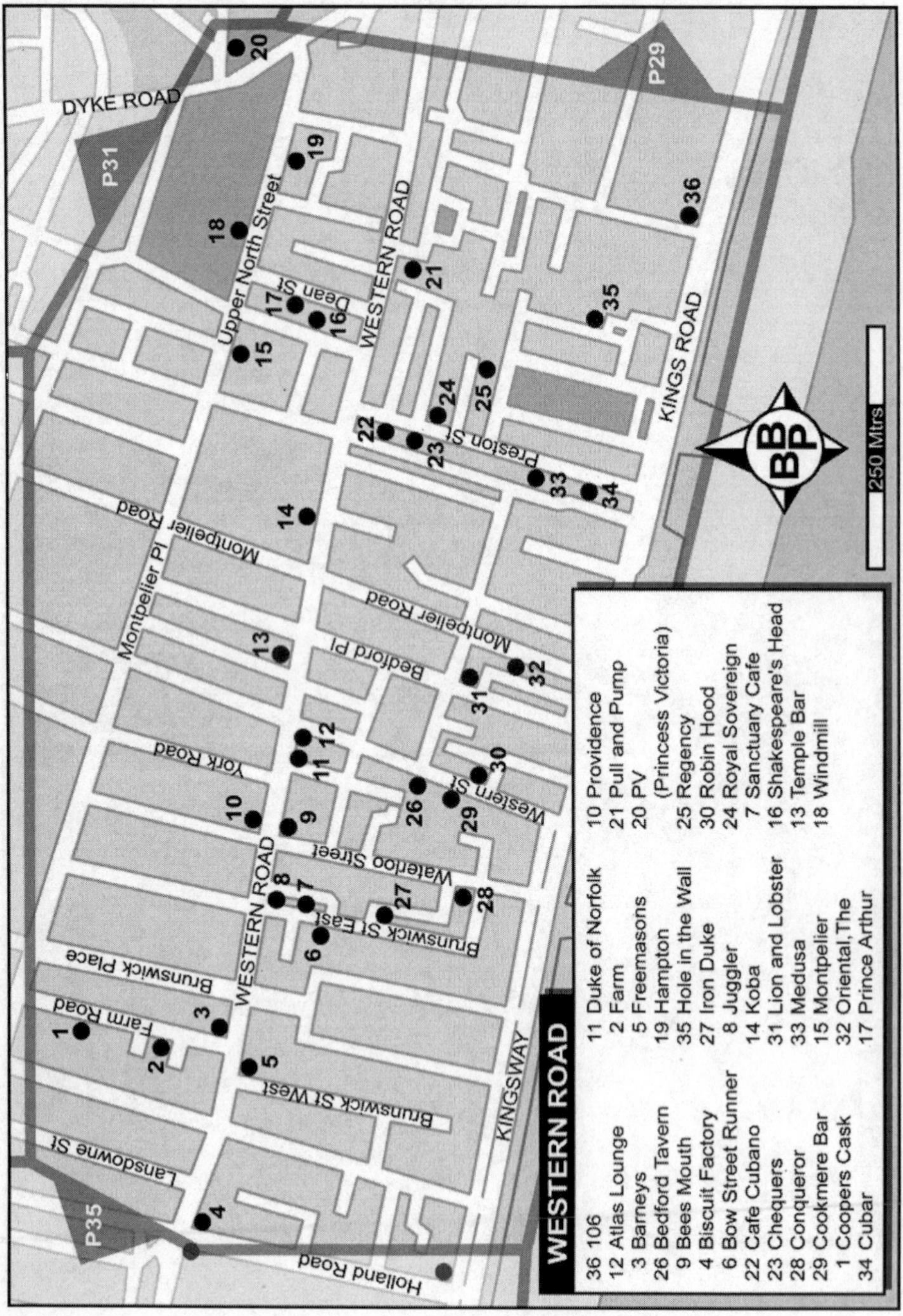
WESTERN ROAD
36 106
12 Atlas Lounge
3 Barneys
26 Bedford Tavern
9 Bees Mouth
4 Biscuit Factory
6 Bow Street Runner
22 Cafe Cubano
23 Chequers
28 Conqueror
29 Cookmere Bar
1 Coopers Cask
34 Cubar
11 Duke of Norfolk
2 Farm
5 Freemasons
19 Hampton
35 Hole in the Wall
27 Iron Duke
8 Juggler
14 Koba
31 Lion and Lobster
33 Medusa
15 Montpelier
32 Oriental, The
17 Prince Arthur
10 Providence
21 Pull and Pump
20 PV
(Princess Victoria)
25 Regency
30 Robin Hood
24 Royal Sovereign
7 Sanctuary Cafe
16 Shakespeare's Head
13 Temple Bar
18 Windmill
DYKE ROAD
Upper North Street
Dean St
WESTERN ROAD
Preston St
KINGS ROAD
Montpelier Road
Montpelier Pl
Bedford Pl
York Road
Western St
Waterloo Street
Brunswick St East
Brunswick Place
Farm Road
Brunswick St West
Lansdowne St
Holland Road
KINGSWAY
P31
P29
P35
250 Mtrs

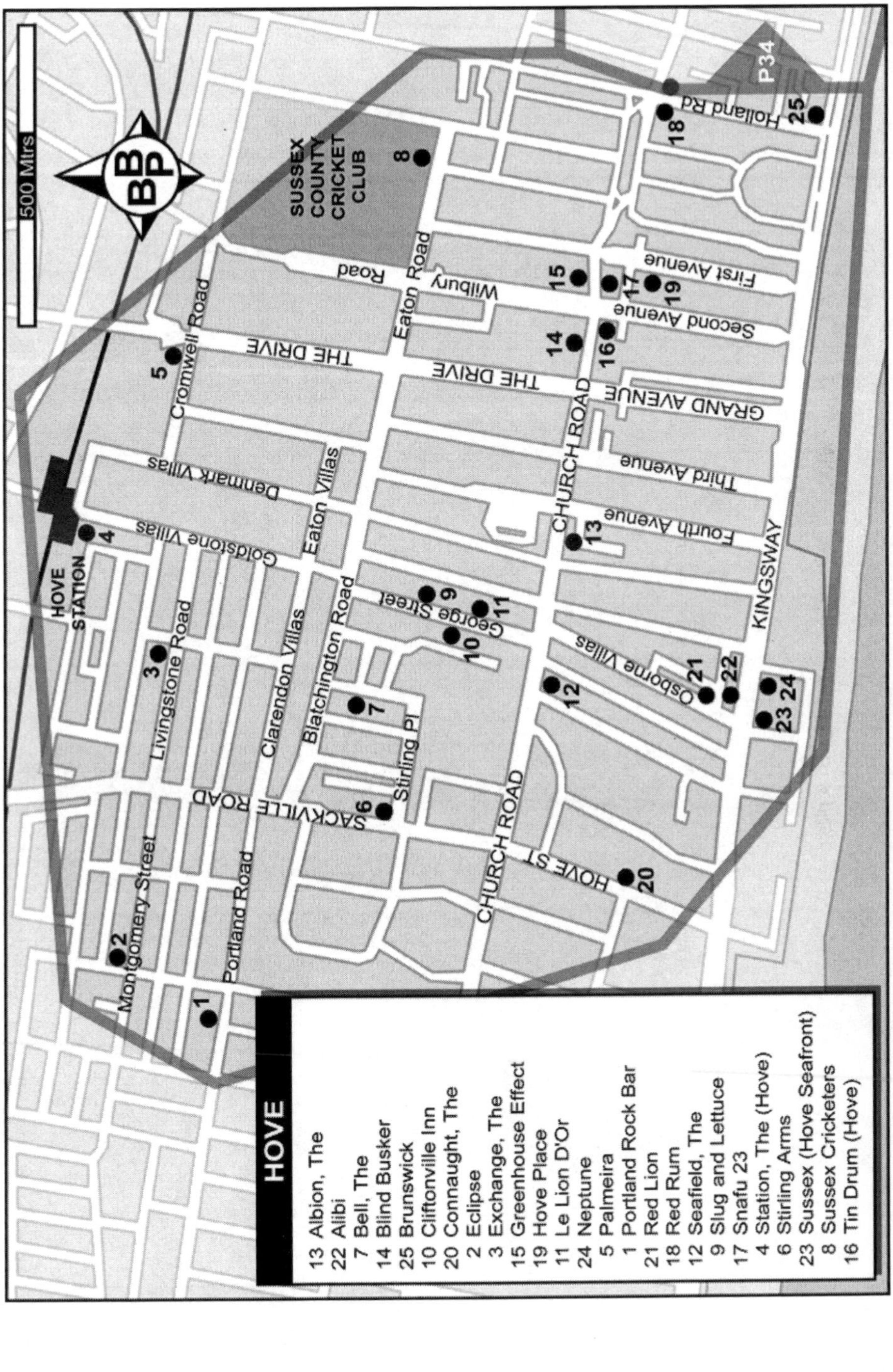
HOVE
13 Albion, The
22 Alibi
7 Bell, The
14 Blind Busker
25 Brunswick
10 Cliftonville Inn
20 Connaught, The
2 Eclipse
3 Exchange, The
15 Greenhouse Effect
19 Hove Place
11 Le Lion D'Or
24 Neptune
5 Palmeira
1 Portland Rock Bar
21 Red Lion
18 Red Rum
12 Seafield, The
9 Slug and Lettuce
17 Snafu 23
4 Station, The (Hove)
6 Stirling Arms
23 Sussex (Hove Seafront)
8 Sussex Cricketers
16 Tin Drum (Hove)
500 Mtrs
SUSSEX COUNTY CRICKET CLUB
HOVE STATION
Cromwell Road
THE DRIVE
Eaton Road
Wilbury Road
First Avenue
Second Avenue
GRAND AVENUE
Third Avenue
Fourth Avenue
CHURCH ROAD
KINGSWAY
Holland Rd
Denmark Villas
Goldstone Villas
Eaton Villas
George Street
Osborne Villas
Livingstone Road
Clarendon Villas
Blatchington Road
Stirling Pl
SACKVILLE ROAD
HOVE ST
Montgomery Street
Portland Road
P34

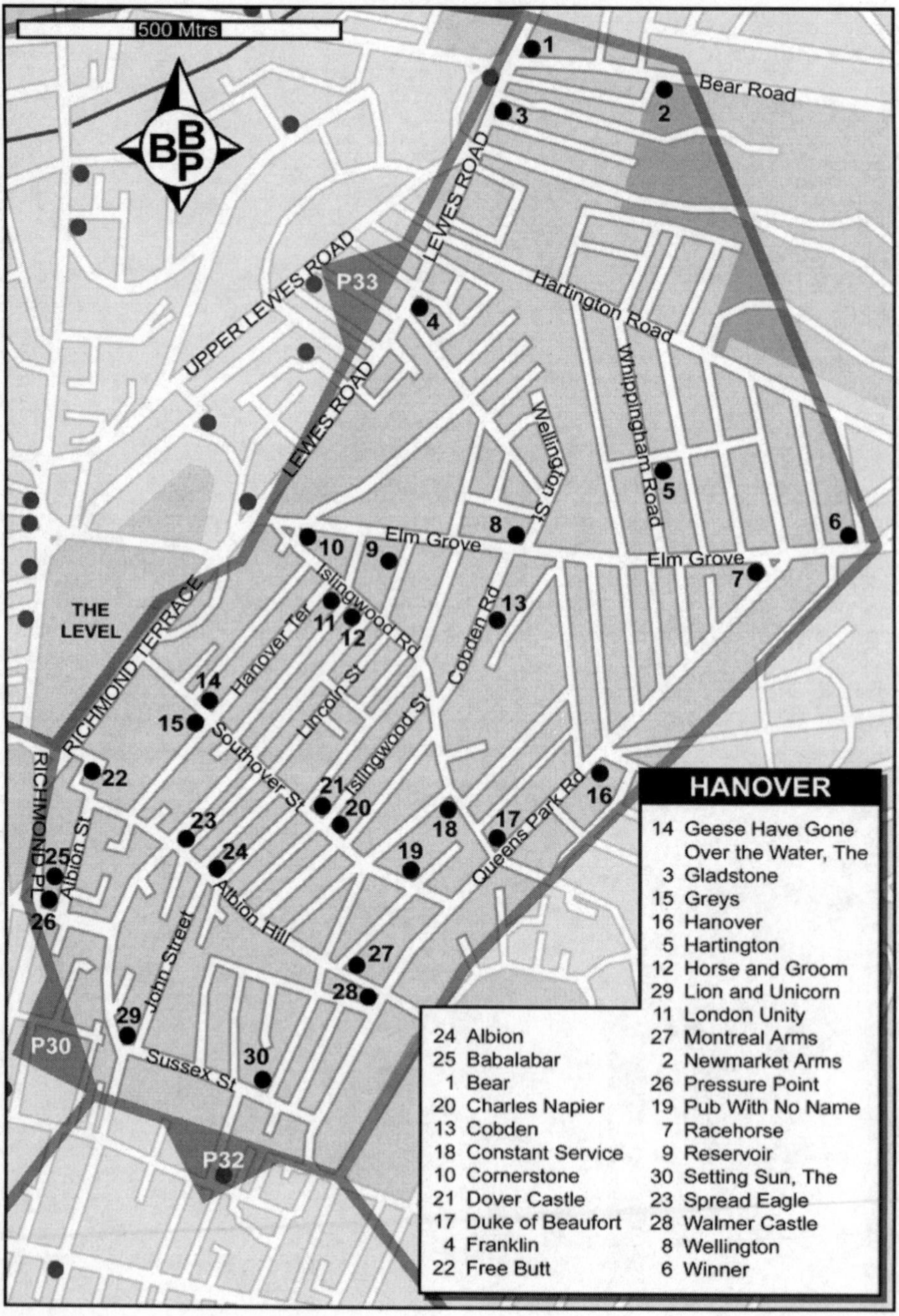
500 Mtrs
Bear Road
LEWES ROAD
UPPER LEWES ROAD
P33
Hartington Road
Whippingham Road
Wellington St
Elm Grove
Elm Grove
THE LEVEL
RICHMOND TERRACE
Hanover Ter
Islingwood Rd
Cobden Rd
Lincoln St
Islingwood St
Southover St
Queens Park Rd
RICHMOND PL
Albion St
Albion Hill
John Street
Sussex St
P30
P32
HANOVER
24 Albion
25 Babalabar
1 Bear
20 Charles Napier
13 Cobden
18 Constant Service
10 Cornerstone
21 Dover Castle
17 Duke of Beaufort
4 Franklin
22 Free Butt
14 Geese Have Gone Over the Water, The
3 Gladstone
15 Greys
16 Hanover
5 Hartington
12 Horse and Groom
29 Lion and Unicorn
11 London Unity
27 Montreal Arms
2 Newmarket Arms
26 Pressure Point
19 Pub With No Name
7 Racehorse
9 Reservoir
30 Setting Sun, The
23 Spread Eagle
28 Walmer Castle
8 Wellington
6 Winner

106

49%
Pub Rating

Street: Under the Metropole Hotel
Area of Brighton: Seafront
Pub Type: Pre-club

Atmosphere	Beer	Barstaff	Food	Entertainment	Décor/Garden
38%	**46%**	**46%**	**54%**	**33%**	**58%**

All day bar/pub attached to the Metropole. Pleasant sea views from an elevated, protected position.

14

68%
Pub Rating

Street: Ship Street
Area of Brighton: Lanes
Pub Type: Pre-club

Atmosphere	Beer	Barstaff	Food	Entertainment	Décor/Garden
50%	**63%**	**75%**	**31%**	**38%**	**75%**

Very swish looking café-bar with buckets of style. Opened March 2003 as "Galore" and changed its name to "14" for no apparent reason.

Albion (Hanover)

54%
Pub Rating

Street: Albion Hill
Area of Brighton: Hanover
Pub Type: Local

Atmosphere	Beer	Barstaff	Food	Entertainment	Décor/Garden
28%	**63%**	**53%**	**38%**	**59%**	**56%**

Well-kept and professionally run locals' pub. Traditional decor with 2 bar billiards tables & dart board. Lots of tongue & groove. Not very exciting.

Albion , The (Hove)

58%
Pub Rating

Street: Church Road
Area of Brighton: Hove
Pub Type: Local

Atmosphere	Beer	Barstaff	Food	Entertainment	Décor/Garden
44%	**59%**	**44%**	**53%**	**53%**	**53%**

Spacious, conventional, boring town centre pub with "Are you a local ?" attitude and TV football. Pub Quiz alternate Sundays.

Ali Cats

82%
Pub Rating

Street: East Street (Under the Prodigal)
Area of Brighton: Lanes
Pub Type: Pre-club & Studenty

Atmosphere	Beer	Barstaff	Food	Entertainment	Décor/Garden
79%	**54%**	**68%**	**39%**	**79%**	**57%**

Basement dive with sofas, good atmosphere and homemade bowling lane. Shows films in the afternoon.

Alibi

61%
Pub Rating

Street: St Catherines Terrace
Area of Brighton: Hove
Pub Type: Town

Atmosphere	Beer	Barstaff	Food	Entertainment	Décor/Garden
54%	**50%**	**46%**	**46%**	**46%**	**63%**

Large traditional pub near Hove seafront. Has recently been refurbished with a new lounge and beer garden. Roasts on a Sunday and barbaques twice a week. Pool Table. Surfer wannabees hang out here.

Amsterdam

61%
Pub Rating

Street: Marine Parade
Area of Brighton: St. James' Street
Pub Type: Gay & Town

Atmosphere	Beer	Barstaff	Food	Entertainment	Décor/Garden
53%	**53%**	**44%**	**38%**	**44%**	**69%**

Smart, trendy seafront pub, hilariously gay. Possesses a sauna complex and jacuzzi. Specialist cocktails available, like a Blow Job or a Quick Shag!

Aquarium

55%
Pub Rating

Street: Steine Street
Area of Brighton: St. James' Street
Pub Type: Gay

Atmosphere	Beer	Barstaff	Food	Entertainment	Décor/Garden
44%	**63%**	**63%**	**25%**	**38%**	**44%**

Seedy back street very male gay pub. Unwelcoming for women. Cruisy atmosphere - good chance of being chatted up for men.

Arc

55%
Pub Rating

Street: Kings Road Arches
Area of Brighton: Seafront
Pub Type: Pre-club

Atmosphere	Beer	Barstaff	Food	Entertainment	Décor/Garden
50%	**47%**	**50%**	**38%**	**38%**	**56%**

Cold beer supplying joint on the seafront. Becomes a club later. Cheaper than most of these places. Renamed from Cuba, no other obvious change.

Seafront bar Arc in the Summer

Atlas Lounge

71%
Pub Rating

Street: Western Road
Area of Brighton: Western Road
Pub Type: Town & Studenty

Atmosphere	Beer	Barstaff	Food	Entertainment	Décor/Garden
63%	**50%**	**50%**	**75%**	**50%**	**75%**

Morrocon style café bar, no draught ales, but chilled out, interesting looking menu and games on offer (backgammon, chess, scrabble, battleships). Live music some nights.

Babalabar

38%
Pub Rating

Street: Albion St
Area of Brighton: Hanover
Pub Type: Local

Atmosphere	Beer	Barstaff	Food	Entertainment	Décor/Garden
29%	**38%**	**42%**	**21%**	**50%**	**38%**

Awful kiddy disco bar. Pool tables, live DJs, TV screens. Not enough to distract you from the other customers though. (Currently made "student only" which may make it worse/better depending on how you feel about students).

Bacchus Bar

56%
Pub Rating

Street: Albert Street
Area of Brighton: Lanes
Pub Type: Town

Atmosphere	Beer	Barstaff	Food	Entertainment	Décor/Garden
50%	**63%**	**54%**	**0%**	**8%**	**75%**

Expensive but pleasant wine bar. Personal service, fish tank in the ceiling and a stannah stair lift.....

Bar de la Mer

51%
Pub Rating

Street: Kings Road Arches
Area of Brighton: Seafront
Pub Type: Town

Atmosphere	Beer	Barstaff	Food	Entertainment	Décor/Garden
56%	**31%**	**31%**	**50%**	**50%**	**50%**

Seafront stall masquerading as a bar. Tables for that authentic 'I'm having a beer on holiday' feel. Nice view of the volleyball court. More tables on the roof.....

Bar Rogue

55%
Pub Rating

Street: Kings Road
Area of Brighton: Lanes
Pub Type: Town

Atmosphere	Beer	Barstaff	Food	Entertainment	Décor/Garden
46%	**38%**	**42%**	**50%**	**42%**	**75%**

Flashy new place near the pier. Drinks deals, sofas and a huge TV. Not too much appeal otherwise.

Bar Valentine

77%
Pub Rating

Street: New Road
Area of Brighton: North Laine
Pub Type: Cocktail

Atmosphere	Beer	Barstaff	Food	Entertainment	Décor/Garden
75%	**67%**	**67%**	**33%**	**29%**	**71%**

Relaxed, cool, cocktail bar with reasonably priced cocktails, nice music and friendly barstaff.

Barley Mow

63%
Pub Rating

Street: St George's Road
Area of Brighton: Kemptown
Pub Type: Local & Studenty

Atmosphere	Beer	Barstaff	Food	Entertainment	Décor/Garden
56%	**50%**	**59%**	**44%**	**47%**	**56%**

Pleasant , friendly, well-stocked pub in the middle of Kemptown. Pub Quiz on a Thursday.

The Barley Mow, a popular local's pub in Kemptown

Barneys

50%
Pub Rating

Street: Western Road
Area of Brighton: Western Road
Pub Type: Town

Atmosphere	Beer	Barstaff	Food	Entertainment	Décor/Garden
38%	**44%**	**47%**	**75%**	**22%**	**69%**

Posey bar/restaurant/beer on the street place right on Western Road.

Basketmakers Arms, The

94%
Pub Rating

Street: Gloucester Road
Area of Brighton: North Laine
Pub Type: Town

Atmosphere	Beer	Barstaff	Food	Entertainment	Décor/Garden
82%	**96%**	**61%**	**89%**	**32%**	**71%**

Friendly pub usually packed to the gunnels, with good food, beer and weird wines. No machines. Interesting messages in the antique tobacco tin collection on the walls.....

The Basketmakers – possibly the best pub in Brighton, in the North Laine

Bat & Ball

35%
Pub Rating

Street: Oxford Place
Area of Brighton: Ditchling Road
Pub Type: Local

Atmosphere	Beer	Barstaff	Food	Entertainment	Décor/Garden
23%	**43%**	**45%**	**25%**	**53%**	**28%**

Only to be entered for the quiz, cheap drink or when plastered to watch televised football.

The Bat & Ball – rather overdoing it with the flower baskets

Bath Arms

56%
Pub Rating

Street: Union Street
Area of Brighton: Lanes
Pub Type: Town

Atmosphere	Beer	Barstaff	Food	Entertainment	Décor/Garden
52%	**56%**	**42%**	**42%**	**46%**	**42%**

Standard pub, but hidden in the Lanes. Apparently got a talking parrot. Good selection of beer, poor selection of barstaff. Pub Quiz on a Tuesday.

Battle of Trafalgar

79%
Pub Rating

Street: Guildford Rd
Area of Brighton: Seven Dials
Pub Type: Town

Atmosphere	Beer	Barstaff	Food	Entertainment	Décor/Garden
68%	**71%**	**59%**	**63%**	**43%**	**70%**

U-shaped, traditional, town pub . Nice garden, very comfortable. Refuses to offer vinegar because it 'makes the beer go flat'!

The Battle of Trafalgar prides itself on its beer

Beach

55%
Pub Rating

Street: Kings Road Arches
Area of Brighton: Seafront
Pub Type: Pre-club

Atmosphere	Beer	Barstaff	Food	Entertainment	Décor/Garden
48%	**45%**	**45%**	**53%**	**40%**	**63%**

Bar thats really a big beat club later. Hang out on the beach during the day.

Bear

60%
Pub Rating

Street: The Gyratory
Area of Brighton: Hanover
Pub Type: Local & Studenty

Atmosphere	Beer	Barstaff	Food	Entertainment	Décor/Garden
53%	**58%**	**48%**	**45%**	**55%**	**45%**

Locals pub, okay for a chat and special offers for students

Bedford Tavern

65%
Pub Rating

Street: Western Street
Area of Brighton: Western Road
Pub Type: Local

Atmosphere	Beer	Barstaff	Food	Entertainment	Décor/Garden
50%	**72%**	**59%**	**38%**	**41%**	**56%**

Friendly traditional pub near the seafront. Gay-friendly. Tolkien pictures. LAGRAD meetings (!).

The Bedford Tavern, south of Western Road, appeals to a wide range of punters!

Bees Mouth, The

82%
Pub Rating

Street: Western Road
Area of Brighton: Western Road
Pub Type: Town

Atmosphere	Beer	Barstaff	Food	Entertainment	Décor/Garden
75%	**50%**	**75%**	**13%**	**75%**	**75%**

A bar with real character and a very strong smell of incense. Its own little gallery, live music most nights and friendly barstaff. Interesting lagers on tap, cocktails and proper coffee on offer.

Bell, The

38%
Pub Rating

Street: Belfast Street
Area of Brighton: Hove
Pub Type: Local

Atmosphere	Beer	Barstaff	Food	Entertainment	Décor/Garden
38%	**50%**	**25%**	**0%**	**25%**	**50%**

Smoke-filled, slovenly locals' pub. Off the beaten track, so you're unlikely to find it; don't waste your time and money.

Belle Vue

73%
Pub Rating

Street: Buckingham Place
Area of Brighton: Seven Dials
Pub Type: Town

Atmosphere	Beer	Barstaff	Food	Entertainment	Décor/Garden
55%	**59%**	**64%**	**57%**	**57%**	**71%**

Interesting pictures, friendly barstaff and comfy chairs with a great view. Also table football if you are feeling sporty.

Biscuit Factory

59%
Pub Rating

Street: Western Road
Area of Brighton: Western Road
Pub Type: Town

Atmosphere	Beer	Barstaff	Food	Entertainment	Décor/Garden
50%	**44%**	**50%**	**50%**	**46%**	**69%**

What a loss this was. First this was the Wick Inn, which was transformed into Nan Tuks, Brightons only gothic pub, only to be turned into this plastic monstrosity of a bar. Hideous.

Black Horse (Kemptown)

58%
Pub Rating

Street: Montague Place
Area of Brighton: Kemptown
Pub Type: Local

Atmosphere	Beer	Barstaff	Food	Entertainment	Décor/Garden
50%	**44%**	**69%**	**25%**	**31%**	**69%**

Completely refurbished from the old Black Horse in March 2003. Boarded floors and friendly barstaff with a slightly continental feel. Mysteriously empty of customers, perhaps the previous regulars are snubbing it because of the total change.

Black Horse (North Laine)

62%
Pub Rating

Street: Church Street
Area of Brighton: North Laine
Pub Type: Gay & Town

Atmosphere	Beer	Barstaff	Food	Entertainment	Décor/Garden
58%	**53%**	**65%**	**35%**	**40%**	**50%**

Tedious pub, okay for a quiet drink, big back room.
Under new management in April 2006, who seem to be making improvements.

Black Lion (Lanes)

52%
Pub Rating

Street: Black Lion Street
Area of Brighton: Lanes
Pub Type: Pre-club

Atmosphere	Beer	Barstaff	Food	Entertainment	Décor/Garden
50%	**50%**	**40%**	**50%**	**45%**	**38%**

Unfriendly atmosphere but good if you are up for a clubby night out

Black Lion (Patcham)

53%
Pub Rating

Street: A23
Area of Brighton: North Brighton
Pub Type: Town

Atmosphere	Beer	Barstaff	Food	Entertainment	Décor/Garden
33%	**50%**	**42%**	**58%**	**46%**	**71%**

A very big Beefeater style pub. Unmissable when you drive into Brighton, just after the A23 roundabout

Blanch House

65%
Pub Rating

Street: Atlingworth Street
Area of Brighton: Kemptown
Pub Type: Cocktail

Atmosphere	Beer	Barstaff	Food	Entertainment	Décor/Garden
50%	**38%**	**75%**	**75%**	**25%**	**88%**

"Exclusive", "Celebrity" bar and restaurant. Entry via buzzer system. Either you are desperate to get there or desperate to demolish it. Looks fantastic inside and has won shining reviews from journalists.

Blind Busker

66%
Pub Rating

Street: Church Road
Area of Brighton: Hove
Pub Type: Town

Atmosphere	Beer	Barstaff	Food	Entertainment	Décor/Garden
50%	**85%**	**48%**	**53%**	**35%**	**55%**

Lively, central and popular pub with superb selection of draft beers and some Belgian bottled beers on offer

Boardwalk

65%
Pub Rating

Street: Kings Road Arches
Area of Brighton: Seafront
Pub Type: Town

Atmosphere	Beer	Barstaff	Food	Entertainment	Décor/Garden
58%	**25%**	**58%**	**71%**	**29%**	**100%**

Cool tunes and a good view of the beach and pier. Nice coffee and food, limited draft beer. Newspapers available Shame about the slow service.

Bombay Bar

74%
Pub Rating

Street: St George's Road
Area of Brighton: Kemptown
Pub Type: Pre-club

Atmosphere	Beer	Barstaff	Food	Entertainment	Décor/Garden
75%	**31%**	**50%**	**50%**	**81%**	**69%**

Attached to the Hanbury Arms and a big contrast. Open on a Friday or Saturday with bands & DJ. £5 to get in and open till 2pm. Jazz on a Monday till 2pm. Really cool atmosphere, expensive drinks.

Bonaparte's

34%
Pub Rating

Street: In the Station
Area of Brighton: North Laine
Pub Type: Town

Atmosphere	Beer	Barstaff	Food	Entertainment	Décor/Garden
25%	**33%**	**50%**	**33%**	**25%**	**46%**

Better than average station bar, but that's all it is. You're mad if you are in here for more than one drink.

Bow Street Runner

36%
Pub Rating

Street: Brunswick Street
Area of Brighton: Western Road
Pub Type: Town

Atmosphere	Beer	Barstaff	Food	Entertainment	Décor/Garden
28%	**50%**	**47%**	**25%**	**31%**	**25%**

Small, smokey, mediocre at the back end of Western road. Entertainment is a charity book sale. Dogs welcome!

Branch Tavern

48%
Pub Rating

Street: London Road
Area of Brighton: Ditchling Road
Pub Type: Local

Atmosphere	Beer	Barstaff	Food	Entertainment	Décor/Garden
28%	**56%**	**50%**	**25%**	**66%**	**41%**

Below average town pub, popular with the locals, best advice is to leave it to them.

Brewer's Tap

61%
Pub Rating

Street: London Road
Area of Brighton: North Brighton
Pub Type: Local

Atmosphere	Beer	Barstaff	Food	Entertainment	Décor/Garden
42%	**54%**	**54%**	**54%**	**67%**	**58%**

Smart Preston Village pub with good range of beers and entertainments. Popular with local youngsters :-(

Bright Helm, The

47%
Pub Rating

Street: West Street
Area of Brighton: Clock Tower
Pub Type: Town

Atmosphere	Beer	Barstaff	Food	Entertainment	Décor/Garden
30%	**80%**	**35%**	**33%**	**35%**	**35%**

Large selection of very cheap beer, otherwise like drinking in an airport bar - loads of people but no atmosphere. The Wetherspoons trademarks are all here, including no music.

Brighton Rocks

61%
Pub Rating

Street: Rock Place
Area of Brighton: St. James' Street
Pub Type: Town & Local

Atmosphere	Beer	Barstaff	Food	Entertainment	Décor/Garden
56%	**50%**	**56%**	**63%**	**31%**	**56%**

Bright, refurbished, traditional pub near to seafront. Good food on offer.

Brighton Tavern

56%
Pub Rating

Street: Gloucester Road
Area of Brighton: North Laine
Pub Type: Local

Atmosphere	Beer	Barstaff	Food	Entertainment	Décor/Garden
44%	**53%**	**56%**	**41%**	**41%**	**56%**

Lots of interesting things to look at with a pleasant atmostphere. Pin Ball machine in the dingier bar. Allegedly full of antique dealers. Can be quiet and boring.

Bristol Bar

61%
Pub Rating

Street: Kings Road
Area of Brighton: Kemptown
Pub Type: Town

Atmosphere	Beer	Barstaff	Food	Entertainment	Décor/Garden
50%	**54%**	**50%**	**50%**	**50%**	**58%**

Standard pub - pool table and nice view of the sea. Sometimes a bit of a sports/football pub.

Browns

50%
Pub Rating

Street: Dukes Lane
Area of Brighton: Lanes
Pub Type: Town

Atmosphere	Beer	Barstaff	Food	Entertainment	Décor/Garden
44%	**38%**	**47%**	**66%**	**25%**	**63%**

Posh bar with draughts set. Ideal for a G 'n' T, otherwise steer clear.

Brunswick

60%
Pub Rating

Street: Holland Road
Area of Brighton: Hove
Pub Type: Town

Atmosphere	Beer	Barstaff	Food	Entertainment	Décor/Garden
42%	**54%**	**52%**	**54%**	**75%**	**48%**

Big bizzarely decorated (as American/sports/traditional) pub, lots of pool tables, regular live music, also shows live football and tries to get the atmosphere going with theme nights - shame the regulars are so dull

Buddies

59%
Pub Rating

Street: Kings Road
Area of Brighton: Seafront
Pub Type: Town

Atmosphere	Beer	Barstaff	Food	Entertainment	Décor/Garden
50%	**50%**	**50%**	**75%**	**75%**	**25%**

Bar for backpackers right on the Kings Road. But why drink here by a busy road when you could be on the beach? Famous for serving food 24 hours a day.

Buddies Bar - Under Brighton Backpackers on the Kings Road

Bugle

76%
Pub Rating

Street: St Martin's St
Area of Brighton: Ditchling Road
Pub Type: Irish & Local

Atmosphere	Beer	Barstaff	Food	Entertainment	Décor/Garden
67%	**75%**	**52%**	**29%**	**58%**	**58%**

Real Irish pub with live music and good Guinness. Locals, students, Irish and bikers mingle in a relaxed manner. Large, wild beer garden out the back.

Bulldog

58%
Pub Rating

Street: St. James' Street
Area of Brighton: St. James' Street
Pub Type: Gay

Atmosphere	Beer	Barstaff	Food	Entertainment	Décor/Garden
63%	**38%**	**50%**	**50%**	**38%**	**50%**

Very Lively Kemptown gay club. Maybe too lively for your average straight person!

Café Cubano

69%
Pub Rating

Street: Preston Street
Area of Brighton: Western Road
Pub Type: Town

Atmosphere	Beer	Barstaff	Food	Entertainment	Décor/Garden
75%	**50%**	**50%**	**50%**	**75%**	**25%**

Cuban style bar/café with lots of rum-based cuban cocktails, bottled beer, cuban coffee, snack food and salsa music. Overflowing onto the street when we visited on a Saturday. Opened January 2003.

Candy Bar

61%
Pub Rating

Street: St. James' Street
Area of Brighton: St. James' Street
Pub Type: Pre-Club

Atmosphere	Beer	Barstaff	Food	Entertainment	Décor/Garden
56%	**31%**	**50%**	**44%**	**63%**	**69%**

Second and much improved subterranean location of the strongly lesbian late-night bar/club.

Caxton Arms

81%
Pub Rating

Street: North Gardens
Area of Brighton: Seven Dials
Pub Type: Local & Town

Atmosphere	Beer	Barstaff	Food	Entertainment	Décor/Garden
69%	**65%**	**52%**	**46%**	**67%**	**79%**

Packed lounge, chilled out bar and cool balconey/garden. However, expensive and less than the sum of its parts. A bit more effort and this would be a great pub

Charles Napier

72%
Pub Rating

Street: Southover Street
Area of Brighton: Hanover
Pub Type: Local

Atmosphere	Beer	Barstaff	Food	Entertainment	Décor/Garden
56%	**71%**	**60%**	**48%**	**44%**	**67%**

Decptively large and slightly shabby but well-run traditional pub filled with intriguing historical junk. Great Gales bitters and a lovely garden with pillarbox and beautiful plants

Charles St

60%
Pub Rating

Street: Marine Parade
Area of Brighton: Seafront
Pub Type: Gay

Atmosphere	Beer	Barstaff	Food	Entertainment	Décor/Garden
56%	**50%**	**50%**	**0%**	**38%**	**75%**

Enormous, modern gay bar close to the seafront. A bit like sitting in the Star Ship Enterprise. Poshest toilets in Brighton.

Chequers

43%
Pub Rating

Street: Preston Street
Area of Brighton: Western Road
Pub Type: Local

Atmosphere	Beer	Barstaff	Food	Entertainment	Décor/Garden
44%	**44%**	**50%**	**25%**	**25%**	**38%**

Completely refurbished from being an old folks boozer to a new white-look pub, sure to pull in pre and post scoffers from the Preston St Restaurants

Chez Nous

80%
Pub Rating

Street: Arundel Road
Area of Brighton: Kemptown
Pub Type: Local

Atmosphere	Beer	Barstaff	Food	Entertainment	Décor/Garden
63%	**63%**	**75%**	**50%**	**75%**	**63%**

Big lively local pub with friendly barstaff, extensive range of draught beer & large slightly unkempt beer garden. Pool, darts and fruit machines provide the entertainment.

Circus Circus

50%
Pub Rating

Street: Preston Circus
Area of Brighton: Ditchling Road
Pub Type: Town

Atmosphere	Beer	Barstaff	Food	Entertainment	Décor/Garden
40%	**45%**	**55%**	**58%**	**33%**	**53%**

Café bar ideal for a beer before the Duke of Yorks cinema. Looks more like a Habitat store than a pub, though.

Cleveland, The

61%
Pub Rating

Street: Cleveland Rd
Area of Brighton: North Brighton
Pub Type: Local

Atmosphere	Beer	Barstaff	Food	Entertainment	Décor/Garden
63%	**63%**	**63%**	**0%**	**25%**	**50%**

Small locals' pub behind near to Fiveways. Could do with a lick of paint, but well-run and friendly.

Cliftonville Inn

59%
Pub Rating

Street: George Street
Area of Brighton: Hove
Pub Type: Town & Local

Atmosphere	Beer	Barstaff	Food	Entertainment	Décor/Garden
33%	**92%**	**63%**	**58%**	**25%**	**42%**

Very large and popular Wetherspoons pub in the middle of Hove's main shopping area. Excellent choice of ales and food, plus its stunningly cheap. But its like drinking in an airport or station bar. No music.

Club Barracuda

61%
Pub Rating

Street: Kings Road Arches
Area of Brighton: Seafront
Pub Type: Pre-club

Atmosphere	Beer	Barstaff	Food	Entertainment	Décor/Garden
50%	**50%**	**56%**	**50%**	**38%**	**69%**

Cold beer supplying joint on the seafront. Becomes a club later. Cheaper than most of these places.

Coach House

48%
Pub Rating

Street: Middle Street
Area of Brighton: Lanes
Pub Type: Town

Atmosphere	Beer	Barstaff	Food	Entertainment	Décor/Garden
47%	**31%**	**31%**	**69%**	**22%**	**72%**

Little pub tacked onto a restaurant, which overflows into the food eating area when its not meal time. Nice little outside drinking area.

Cobblers Thumb

57%
Pub Rating

Street: New England Road
Area of Brighton: Ditchling Road
Pub Type: Local

Atmosphere	Beer	Barstaff	Food	Entertainment	Décor/Garden
50%	**59%**	**50%**	**54%**	**46%**	**34%**

Friendly dive of a pub; popular with real ale types, decor a messy mixture. Weird mixture of Australian style and junky museum. Pub Quiz on a Tuesday.

Eclectic décor in the Cobbler's Thumb, near Preston Circus

Cobden

47%
Pub Rating

Street: Cobden Road
Area of Brighton: Hanover
Pub Type: Local

Atmosphere	Beer	Barstaff	Food	Entertainment	Décor/Garden
38%	**44%**	**50%**	**38%**	**38%**	**50%**

Dull, nearly lifeless local's pub. Beer garden and pool table but more people needed.

Collonade Bar

55%
Pub Rating

Street: New Road
Area of Brighton: North Laine
Pub Type: Town

Atmosphere	Beer	Barstaff	Food	Entertainment	Décor/Garden
50%	**50%**	**46%**	**46%**	**38%**	**54%**

Arty, tatty bar next to the Theatre Royal. Handy for interval drinks.

Connaught, The

45%
Pub Rating

Street: Hove Street
Area of Brighton: Hove
Pub Type: Local

Atmosphere	Beer	Barstaff	Food	Entertainment	Décor/Garden
38%	**38%**	**38%**	**75%**	**50%**	**38%**

Smoke-filled, dour pub which could be so much better with a bit of effort. Disappointing. Has a beer garden, apparently.

The Conqueror is a far superior pub after its makeover

Conqueror

61%
Pub Rating

Street: Lower Market St
Area of Brighton: Western Road
Pub Type: Town

Atmosphere	Beer	Barstaff	Food	Entertainment	Décor/Garden
60%	**50%**	**45%**	**38%**	**35%**	**63%**

Back street, central pub, was not very welcoming until it was done up into a trendy bar, quite cool now.

Constant Service

72%
Pub Rating

Street: Islingwood Road
Area of Brighton: Hanover
Pub Type: Local

Atmosphere	Beer	Barstaff	Food	Entertainment	Décor/Garden
63%	**65%**	**68%**	**40%**	**35%**	**70%**

Big single room bar which can have a great atmosphere with beer garden and amazing curved doors

Cookmere Bar

41%
Pub Rating

Street: Western Street
Area of Brighton: Western Road
Pub Type: Town & Local

Atmosphere	Beer	Barstaff	Food	Entertainment	Décor/Garden
29%	**38%**	**50%**	**33%**	**50%**	**42%**

Quite friendly and raved about in the book "Breakfast in Brighton", its changed ownership (and name from Grosvenor Arms) since the book was published.

Coopers Cask

80%
Pub Rating

Street: Farm Road
Area of Brighton: Western Road
Pub Type: Studenty

Atmosphere	Beer	Barstaff	Food	Entertainment	Décor/Garden
75%	**66%**	**63%**	**69%**	**31%**	**72%**

Lively pub just behind the Western Road. Youngish crowd, good range of beers, but rather cramped. A good atmosphere and worth a look if you're in the area. Good food, interesting decor with paintings on the ceiling and sharks over the bar.

Cornerstone

65%
Pub Rating

Street: Elm Grove
Area of Brighton: Hanover
Pub Type: Local

Atmosphere	Beer	Barstaff	Food	Entertainment	Décor/Garden
59%	**47%**	**63%**	**44%**	**38%**	**69%**

Aptly named because of its corner location. The sunlight probably makes it a nicer place than it really is, but the relaxed atmosphere and chilled out music help.

Couch, The

29%
Pub Rating

Street: Dyke Road
Area of Brighton: Seven Dials
Pub Type: Local

Atmosphere	Beer	Barstaff	Food	Entertainment	Décor/Garden
25%	**41%**	**31%**	**13%**	**41%**	**25%**

Although originally a vast improvement on the terrible "Compton Arms" which it replaced, this bar has now backslid and is now not to be recommended.

Crave

43%
Pub Rating

Street: West Street
Area of Brighton: Clock Tower
Pub Type: Town

Atmosphere	Beer	Barstaff	Food	Entertainment	Décor/Garden
50%	**25%**	**50%**	**50%**	**0%**	**63%**

Café bar cashes in on the loaded-down shoppers lurching out of Churchill Square. Only Stella on draught.

Crescent

62%
Pub Rating

Street: Clifton Hill
Area of Brighton: Seven Dials
Pub Type: Town

Atmosphere	Beer	Barstaff	Food	Entertainment	Décor/Garden
55%	**57%**	**46%**	**50%**	**54%**	**48%**

Oldest barstaff in town, boardgames and people reading books in hideyholes, a bit yuppyish. Excellent quiz night on a Tuesday and the second Thursday of each month.

When visited by the Jury it had possibly the oldest barstaff in town – but not the worst

Cricketers

72%
Pub Rating

Street: Black Lion Street
Area of Brighton: Lanes
Pub Type: Town

Atmosphere	Beer	Barstaff	Food	Entertainment	Décor/Garden
71%	**63%**	**52%**	**60%**	**38%**	**58%**

Good atmosphere pub in the centre of the Lanes with arty types and loads of chat. Supposedly Brighton's oldest pub (since 1547).

Crown

32%
Pub Rating

Street: Grafton St
Area of Brighton: St. James' Street
Pub Type: Local

Atmosphere	Beer	Barstaff	Food	Entertainment	Décor/Garden
31%	**44%**	**38%**	**0%**	**25%**	**31%**

Dull old duffers' pub in 1980 timewarp

Crown & Anchor

51%
Pub Rating

Street: London Road
Area of Brighton: North Brighton
Pub Type: Local

Atmosphere	Beer	Barstaff	Food	Entertainment	Décor/Garden
38%	**50%**	**50%**	**63%**	**38%**	**50%**

Large pub in Preston Village. Popular with laddish sports fans, but contains an intriguing selection of wines on draught! occasional live bands.

Cubar

54%
Pub Rating

Street: Preston Street
Area of Brighton: Western Road
Pub Type: Town

Atmosphere	Beer	Barstaff	Food	Entertainment	Décor/Garden
41%	**50%**	**59%**	**31%**	**44%**	**56%**

Vaguely South American bar with loud DJ'd music. Good selection of cocktails with some at bargain prices. Lots of bottled lagers. No bitter.

Cuthbert Arms

55%
Pub Rating

Street: Freshfield Road
Area of Brighton: Kemptown
Pub Type: Local

Atmosphere	Beer	Barstaff	Food	Entertainment	Décor/Garden
38%	**63%**	**50%**	**0%**	**50%**	**63%**

Slightly shabby but reasonable locals' pub, with large beer garden

Devils Dyke Tavern

45%
Pub Rating

Street: The Dyke
Area of Brighton: North Brighton
Pub Type: Town

Atmosphere	Beer	Barstaff	Food	Entertainment	Décor/Garden
33%	**50%**	**42%**	**33%**	**29%**	**58%**

Awful pub which relies on its monopoly position to feed tourists and day trippers unedible food, slowly and serve expensive lager to go with it. Bearable if you sit outside.

Devonshire Arms

28%
Pub Rating

Street: Carlton Hill
Area of Brighton: St. James' Street
Pub Type: Local

Atmosphere	Beer	Barstaff	Food	Entertainment	Décor/Garden
19%	**44%**	**38%**	**13%**	**25%**	**38%**

Large, uncared-for pub. Often empty on a Saturday evening which says it all. Not really worth the trouble.

Dorset

62%
Pub Rating

Street: Bond Street
Area of Brighton: North Laine
Pub Type: Town

Atmosphere	Beer	Barstaff	Food	Entertainment	Décor/Garden
63%	**38%**	**50%**	**63%**	**46%**	**60%**

Trendy bar/restaurant with good food, and lots of tables outside in the summer

Dover Castle

67%
Pub Rating

Street: Southover Street
Area of Brighton: Hanover
Pub Type: Local

Atmosphere	Beer	Barstaff	Food	Entertainment	Décor/Garden
60%	**63%**	**54%**	**52%**	**42%**	**56%**

Big single room Hanover pub with garden and interesting beers. Decor and atmosphere much improved since it has 'worn in' a bit. Great selection of really interesting veggie food.

The Dover Castle is one of the many popular locals on Southover Street

Dr. Brightons

63%
Pub Rating

Street: Kings Road
Area of Brighton: Lanes
Pub Type: Gay

Atmosphere	Beer	Barstaff	Food	Entertainment	Décor/Garden
56%	**56%**	**50%**	**50%**	**47%**	**53%**

Relaxed, friendly gay pub on the seafront edge of the Lanes.

Dragon

85%
Pub Rating

Street: St George's Road
Area of Brighton: Kemptown
Pub Type: Studenty & Local

Atmosphere	Beer	Barstaff	Food	Entertainment	Décor/Garden
71%	**71%**	**71%**	**83%**	**42%**	**75%**

This is a hidden gem of a pub at the far end of Kemptown has amazing décor and an interesting group of punters. There is a great and varied food menu.

Druids Arms

71%
Pub Rating

Street: Ditchling Road
Area of Brighton: Ditchling Road
Pub Type: Local

Atmosphere	Beer	Barstaff	Food	Entertainment	Décor/Garden
66%	**57%**	**59%**	**43%**	**43%**	**66%**

Busy on Friday and Saturday nights but nowt to do. Recently become very popular with the studenty crowd.

Druids Head

71%
Pub Rating

Street: Market Street
Area of Brighton: Lanes
Pub Type: Studenty

Atmosphere	Beer	Barstaff	Food	Entertainment	Décor/Garden
63%	**55%**	**59%**	**54%**	**54%**	**64%**

Competes with the Cricketers for the claim to be the oldest pub in Brighton, with a secret smugglers tunnel to the seafront. Some nights you might want to use it to escape.

Duke of Beaufort

59%
Pub Rating

Street: Queen's Park Road
Area of Brighton: Hanover
Pub Type: Local

Atmosphere	Beer	Barstaff	Food	Entertainment	Décor/Garden
46%	**54%**	**50%**	**71%**	**58%**	**46%**

Very large locals' pub, with Thai food and Spanish Tapas Bar

Duke of Norfolk

69%
Pub Rating

Street: Western Road
Area of Brighton: Western Road
Pub Type: Town

Atmosphere	Beer	Barstaff	Food	Entertainment	Décor/Garden
56%	**56%**	**53%**	**53%**	**66%**	**59%**

A complete change from the "Polar" bar that it was into a traditional pub with boardgames, books, papers, proper coffee and real beer. A comfortable, trendy atmosphere and a pleasant place to spend an afternoon or evening and watch the Western Road wildlife go by.

Its one of those pubs which looks better on the outside than it is on the inside

Duke of Wellington

51%
Pub Rating

Street: Upper Gloucester Road
Area of Brighton: Seven Dials
Pub Type: Local

Atmosphere	Beer	Barstaff	Food	Entertainment	Décor/Garden
38%	**50%**	**44%**	**50%**	**53%**	**47%**

Average local boozer. Completely middle-of-the-road.

Dyke Tavern

58%
Pub Rating

Street: Dyke Road
Area of Brighton: Seven Dials
Pub Type: Local

Atmosphere	Beer	Barstaff	Food	Entertainment	Décor/Garden
47%	**50%**	**53%**	**53%**	**63%**	**41%**

Historic, very large but slightly depressing pub on the Dyke Road. Food and drink are both OK, but there is no atmosphere to speak of, except when a big football match is on when Sky Sports worship is essential.

Eagle Bar and Bakery

72%
Pub Rating

Street: Gloucester Road
Area of Brighton: North Laine
Pub Type: Town

Atmosphere	Beer	Barstaff	Food	Entertainment	Décor/Garden
59%	**69%**	**66%**	**75%**	**25%**	**66%**

Completely re-built, thank God, from "A shiny pub full of strange people" to a pub with great beer, food, good atmosphere and barstaff. Sister pub of the Hop Poles (?) possible only complaint (like HP) is the music is too loud - good music though! Pub Quiz on Mondays.

Earth & Stars

68%
Pub Rating

Street: Church Street
Area of Brighton: North Laine
Pub Type: Town

Atmosphere	Beer	Barstaff	Food	Entertainment	Décor/Garden
58%	**63%**	**67%**	**50%**	**25%**	**67%**

Totally Green pub, with Organic beer, wine and food, even organic t-shirts for the bar staff. Its got a neutral carbon footprint, which takes longer to explain than there is space. A good place to visit, with friendly barstaff and tasty, interesting food.

Easy Bar

44%
Pub Rating

Street: Cranbourne St
Area of Brighton: Clock Tower
Pub Type: Town

Atmosphere	Beer	Barstaff	Food	Entertainment	Décor/Garden
38%	**41%**	**44%**	**38%**	**25%**	**59%**

Poncy bar replacing the dire Lamb and Flag and preying on unwary escapees from Churchill Square.

Ebony Room

71%
Pub Rating

Street: Marina
Area of Brighton: Kemptown
Pub Type: Town

Atmosphere	Beer	Barstaff	Food	Entertainment	Décor/Garden
50%	**50%**	**63%**	**75%**	**50%**	**88%**

"Bringing a touch of West End chic and sophistication" to the Marina. Offerring 16 varieties of champagne, private 'Two Ton' tables and a turquoise piano it is obviously not your average pub. With a massive range of spirits, cocktails are a speciality, but drinks are expensive. Outdoor terrace overlooking the road. Late bar at weekends.

Eclipse

56%
Pub Rating

Street: Montgomery Street
Area of Brighton: Hove
Pub Type: Local

Atmosphere	Beer	Barstaff	Food	Entertainment	Décor/Garden
50%	**63%**	**50%**	**0%**	**25%**	**63%**

Recommended to us as an excellent place for real ale, but we found it a very odd place with some of the most dysfunctional customers in the area, and that is saying something. Actually outside the boundaries we set for this guide.

Eddy, The

72%
Pub Rating

Street: Guildford St
Area of Brighton: Seven Dials
Pub Type: Town

Atmosphere	Beer	Barstaff	Food	Entertainment	Décor/Garden
63%	**60%**	**63%**	**56%**	**56%**	**56%**

Trendy as you like with lots of schnapps, a settee, an inconveniently situated pool table a giant surfboard hanging from the roof and was that a video jukebox?

Engineer

67%
Pub Rating

Street: Argyle Road
Area of Brighton: Ditchling Road
Pub Type: Local & Studenty

Atmosphere	Beer	Barstaff	Food	Entertainment	Décor/Garden
58%	**53%**	**63%**	**45%**	**48%**	**65%**

Refurbished back-street pub. Clean and comfortable, but limited range of beers. Bar section with sport on TV and lounge for conversation.

Evening Star

73%
Pub Rating

Street: Surrey Street
Area of Brighton: Seven Dials
Pub Type: Town & Real Ale

Atmosphere	Beer	Barstaff	Food	Entertainment	Décor/Garden
63%	**93%**	**63%**	**40%**	**25%**	**50%**

Attracts CAMRA types, recently refurbished, brews own beers and serves up a vast range of weird real ale.

CAMRA's (Campaign for Real Ale) favourite pub in Brighton

Exchange, The

71%
Pub Rating

Street: Livingstone Road
Area of Brighton: Hove
Pub Type: Local

Atmosphere	Beer	Barstaff	Food	Entertainment	Décor/Garden
63%	**56%**	**69%**	**50%**	**50%**	**56%**

Shabby but amiable football fans' pub in the back streets of Hove. Reasonable beer and food, but the Sky Sports addicts are heavy smokers so be prepared to scrub off the nicotine stains afterwards. Bar billiards. Being completely refurbished June 2003.

Farm

48%
Pub Rating

Street: Farm Road
Area of Brighton: Western Road
Pub Type: Local

Atmosphere	Beer	Barstaff	Food	Entertainment	Décor/Garden
41%	**56%**	**50%**	**47%**	**25%**	**41%**

Cosy locals pub, friendly but has little to offer in terms of atmos or entertainment. Middle-aged version of the nearby Coopers Cask.

Fiddlers Elbow

64%
Pub Rating

Street: Boyces Street
Area of Brighton: Lanes
Pub Type: Irish & Town

Atmosphere	Beer	Barstaff	Food	Entertainment	Décor/Garden
54%	**68%**	**54%**	**43%**	**41%**	**52%**

Lively, friendly Irish pub with good Guinness and a vast selection of Irish memorabilia and junk.

Fishbowl

75%
Pub Rating

Street: East Street
Area of Brighton: Lanes
Pub Type: Studenty

Atmosphere	Beer	Barstaff	Food	Entertainment	Décor/Garden
68%	**55%**	**57%**	**48%**	**39%**	**86%**

Small ZEL pub with no bitter, expensive lager and amazing decor

The Fishbowl is also the highest scoring pub for Totty in Brighton……

Font & Firkin

64%
Pub Rating

Street: Union Street
Area of Brighton: Lanes
Pub Type: Town

Atmosphere	Beer	Barstaff	Food	Entertainment	Décor/Garden
57%	**48%**	**50%**	**54%**	**64%**	**54%**

Unique pub in an old church. No longer has its own range of beers and but has live (too loud) music some nights.

The Font & Firkin is oppositte the Bath Arms in The Lanes

Fortunes of War

74%
Pub Rating

Street: Kings Road Arches
Area of Brighton: Seafront
Pub Type: Town

Atmosphere	Beer	Barstaff	Food	Entertainment	Décor/Garden
68%	**54%**	**48%**	**50%**	**50%**	**82%**

Great for a beer in the summer to drink on the beach. Recently expanded and refurbished, which unfortunately means that a lot of the original character has been lost.

Franklin Tavern

49%
Pub Rating

Street: Lewes Road
Area of Brighton: Hanover
Pub Type: Local & Sport

Atmosphere	Beer	Barstaff	Food	Entertainment	Décor/Garden
35%	**50%**	**48%**	**45%**	**53%**	**43%**

Smokey, spit and sawdust sport-lovers' pub. Can be a dubious atmosphere.

Free Butt

71%
Pub Rating

Street: Phoenix Place
Area of Brighton: Hanover
Pub Type: Studenty & Town

Atmosphere	Beer	Barstaff	Food	Entertainment	Décor/Garden
63%	**50%**	**58%**	**50%**	**79%**	**50%**

Smallish pub which has live music almost every night. Now with the Penthouse bar upstairs serving food.

Freemasons

76%
Pub Rating

Street: Western Road
Area of Brighton: Western Road
Pub Type: Town

Atmosphere	Beer	Barstaff	Food	Entertainment	Décor/Garden
75%	**53%**	**63%**	**63%**	**43%**	**65%**

Spacious and well-kept central pub now with a lively crowd and good music. Amiable but slightly unfocused bar staff. Provides a welcome break from Western Road shopping hell.

Fresh Fields Inn

51%
Pub Rating

Street: Freshfield Road
Area of Brighton: Kemptown
Pub Type: Local

Atmosphere	Beer	Barstaff	Food	Entertainment	Décor/Garden
38%	**56%**	**31%**	**0%**	**69%**	**56%**

Spacious, smokey, dour, very local pub. Extensive beer garden with good view, pool table, darts and, of course, Sky Sports.

Fringe

60%
Pub Rating

Street: Kensington Gardens
Area of Brighton: North Laine
Pub Type: Café Bar

Atmosphere	Beer	Barstaff	Food	Entertainment	Décor/Garden
58%	**33%**	**50%**	**75%**	**25%**	**79%**

Fancy new café bar with good real food and lovely surroundings. Has now bought out the cool balconey bar above.

Full Moon

69%
Pub Rating

Street: Boyces Street
Area of Brighton: Lanes
Pub Type: Studenty

Atmosphere	Beer	Barstaff	Food	Entertainment	Décor/Garden
65%	**52%**	**71%**	**52%**	**29%**	**67%**

Arty, new radical, intellectual feel in lounge type decor. Strong, organic cider but where's the bitter? Pub Quiz on Mondays. Not the original Full Moon which was a really alternative pub with wacky lights and very cool, friendly barstaff.

Garden's

59%
Pub Rating

Street: Kensington Gardens
Area of Brighton: North Laine
Pub Type: Town

Atmosphere	Beer	Barstaff	Food	Entertainment	Décor/Garden
50%	**53%**	**56%**	**63%**	**31%**	**56%**

Much re-vamped from its grungy past, now featuring tasteful music, basic colour scheme and fancy lagers on draught. The strange built-in chippy (why?) has now been removed!

Geese Have Gone Over the Water, The

69%
Pub Rating

Street: Southover Street
Area of Brighton: Hanover
Pub Type: Local

Atmosphere	Beer	Barstaff	Food	Entertainment	Décor/Garden
65%	**63%**	**56%**	**54%**	**40%**	**54%**

Excellent semi-Irish traditional pub but with more than its fair share of loonies.

The Geese is usually well worth the climb up the hill from the Lewes Road

Gemini

59%
Pub Rating

Street: Kings Road Arches
Area of Brighton: Seafront
Pub Type: Pre-club

Atmosphere	Beer	Barstaff	Food	Entertainment	Décor/Garden
54%	**38%**	**54%**	**25%**	**54%**	**67%**

Seafront, dark hole-in-the wall bar. Really nice outside area with tables during the season, with regular live bands. Foreign waiter/waitress table service.

Gemini's seafront bar in the summer

George

69%
Pub Rating

Street: Trafalgar Street
Area of Brighton: North Laine
Pub Type: Town

Atmosphere	Beer	Barstaff	Food	Entertainment	Décor/Garden
59%	**63%**	**55%**	**75%**	**34%**	**63%**

Dark but trendy bar with good vegetarian food available (vegetarian pub of the year 2002). Good range of beers and music. Cramped and popular beer garden. Pub quiz on a Sunday.

Gin Gin

56%
Pub Rating

Street: St. James' Street
Area of Brighton: St. James' Street
Pub Type: Cocktail

Atmosphere	Beer	Barstaff	Food	Entertainment	Décor/Garden
50%	**38%**	**75%**	**0%**	**25%**	**75%**

Stylish cocktail bar decorated by a strange (but not unpleasant) mixture of champagne bottles and religious paintings. Draught lagers, bottled beers, wine and a huge selection of cocktails. All expensive, but the bar claims to have the best Mojitos in town.....

Gladstone

70%
Pub Rating

Street: The Gyratory
Area of Brighton: Hanover
Pub Type: Local & Studenty

Atmosphere	Beer	Barstaff	Food	Entertainment	Décor/Garden
54%	**56%**	**63%**	**46%**	**75%**	**56%**

A pub which has gradually transformed itself into a pseudo-Latin bar. occasional live music, huge garden, daily drinks deals and tapas. Well worth a look now.

Globe, The

70%
Pub Rating

Street: Middle Street
Area of Brighton: Lanes
Pub Type: Town

Atmosphere	Beer	Barstaff	Food	Entertainment	Décor/Garden
69%	**50%**	**59%**	**50%**	**38%**	**69%**

Had a high profile re-launch of a 'proper pub' replacing the Squid bar. It has an interesting theme as a kind of old style colonial gentlemen's club. The food menu is also rather astonishing... "...poached fish of the day on a lemongrass, chilli and coriander risoto, served with saffron cream..."

Golden Cannon

50%
Pub Rating

Street: St George's Road
Area of Brighton: Kemptown
Pub Type: Local

Atmosphere	Beer	Barstaff	Food	Entertainment	Décor/Garden
44%	**56%**	**38%**	**38%**	**38%**	**44%**

Busy pub in the middle of Kemptown

Good Companions

57%
Pub Rating

Street: Dyke Road
Area of Brighton: Seven Dials
Pub Type: Local

Atmosphere	Beer	Barstaff	Food	Entertainment	Décor/Garden
44%	**58%**	**48%**	**46%**	**54%**	**46%**

Standard large boring pub in constant decline

Grand Central

71%
Pub Rating

Street: Surrey Street
Area of Brighton: Seven Dials
Pub Type: Town

Atmosphere	Beer	Barstaff	Food	Entertainment	Décor/Garden
61%	57%	57%	61%	64%	54%

Large sophisticated bar with good food (but pigeon?!), live music, no machines, wine list, breakfasts and the possible re-opening of the Nightingale Theatre upstairs. Secret garden out the back. Was the "Finnegans Wake". Door staff can be obnoxious.

Great Eastern

77%
Pub Rating

Street: Trafalgar Street
Area of Brighton: North Laine
Pub Type: Town & Studenty

Atmosphere	Beer	Barstaff	Food	Entertainment	Décor/Garden
73%	59%	63%	46%	46%	68%

Intimate town bar with wide selection of drinks and food

Greenhouse Effect

62%
Pub Rating

Street: Church Road
Area of Brighton: Hove
Pub Type: Café Bar

Atmosphere	Beer	Barstaff	Food	Entertainment	Décor/Garden
50%	**56%**	**50%**	**53%**	**38%**	**69%**

Interesting place which looks like a poncy bar from the outside and isn't. Great beer, garden, live music and a downstairs which has different bands on. Late night drinking available.

Greens

38%
Pub Rating

Street: West Street
Area of Brighton: Clock Tower
Pub Type: Town & Pre-Club

Atmosphere	Beer	Barstaff	Food	Entertainment	Décor/Garden
29%	**33%**	**50%**	**50%**	**25%**	**50%**

Comfy, noisy, pre-club bar. Some very dubious-looking customers.

Greys

76%
Pub Rating

Street: Southover Street
Area of Brighton: Hanover
Pub Type: Local

Atmosphere	Beer	Barstaff	Food	Entertainment	Décor/Garden
58%	**71%**	**58%**	**71%**	**67%**	**56%**

Drab decor with a limited choice of draught beers, but with speciality Belgian bottled beers, good home cooking ("restaurant quality food" said one juror) and regular live bands

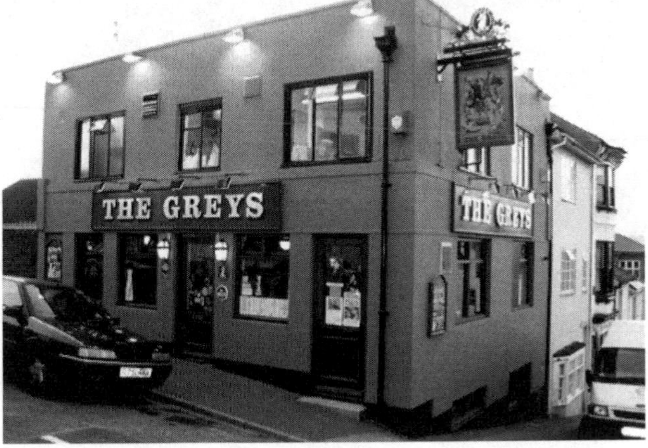

Ha! Ha!

46%
Pub Rating

Street: Pavillion Gardens
Area of Brighton: North Laine
Pub Type: Town

Atmosphere	Beer	Barstaff	Food	Entertainment	Décor/Garden
44%	**34%**	**31%**	**63%**	**25%**	**66%**

Stylish bar with good food and large selection of drinks if you don't want draft beer (which doesn't have a good selection). Newspapers available to read.

Hampton

66%
Pub Rating

Street: Upper North Street
Area of Brighton: Western Road
Pub Type: Local

Atmosphere	Beer	Barstaff	Food	Entertainment	Décor/Garden
63%	**50%**	**50%**	**50%**	**41%**	**69%**

Airy, trendy modern watering hole with "heated garden" (!), cool tunes and zombie barstaff, ideal for young swinger-dingers/lager drinkers. Good and interesting food menu, reasonably priced.

The Hampton is far more stylish than the exterior implies!

Hanbury Arms

44%
Pub Rating

Street: St George's Road
Area of Brighton: Kemptown
Pub Type: Town & Local

Atmosphere	Beer	Barstaff	Food	Entertainment	Décor/Garden
25%	**50%**	**58%**	**50%**	**17%**	**63%**

Well-preserved (nice wood panelling) but gloomy Kemptown pub. Literally a tomb ("Sassoon's Mausoleum"). Small. Attached to the much more lively Bombay Bar.

Hand in Hand

65%
Pub Rating

Street: Upper St. James' Street
Area of Brighton: St. James' Street
Pub Type: Local

Atmosphere	Beer	Barstaff	Food	Entertainment	Décor/Garden
63%	**56%**	**59%**	**38%**	**38%**	**53%**

Small, almost intimate, friendly well-run Kemptown 'brew' pub - brews its own beers. You can't knock the entertainment: you can read the walls. Not sure about the brewed beers, but good lager!

Hanover

78%
Pub Rating

Street: Queen's Park Road
Area of Brighton: Hanover
Pub Type: Town

Atmosphere	Beer	Barstaff	Food	Entertainment	Décor/Garden
67%	71%	75%	67%	13%	79%

Extensive range of lager on draft, but with ale & cider, too. Tasty looking food menu. Tables and décor needs to wear in a little before it loses the cafeteria feel. Very popular already. Seemingly very well run. Excellent Guiness.

Hanrahans

62%
Pub Rating

Street: Marina
Area of Brighton: Kemptown
Pub Type: Town

Atmosphere	Beer	Barstaff	Food	Entertainment	Décor/Garden
50%	54%	54%	50%	33%	75%

Recently refurbished, but still plastic big pub/restaurant in the Marina. Seats outside look over the water and a variety of boats.

Hare & Hounds

43%
Pub Rating

Street: Preston Circus
Area of Brighton: Ditchling Road
Pub Type: Local

Atmosphere	Beer	Barstaff	Food	Entertainment	Décor/Garden
27%	46%	38%	33%	65%	42%

Wasted opportunity, with threatening atmosphere and lots of tellies. Good for live football though.

Harlequins

65%
Pub Rating

Street: Providence Place
Area of Brighton: Ditchling Road
Pub Type: Gay

Atmosphere	Beer	Barstaff	Food	Entertainment	Décor/Garden
50%	68%	48%	50%	60%	50%

Mainly gay, but welcoming multi floor pub/bar. Good selection of beers and stunning selection of customers. Late night drinking available some nights.

Hartington

82%
Pub Rating

Street: Whippingham
Area of Brighton: Hanover
Pub Type: Local

Atmosphere	Beer	Barstaff	Food	Entertainment	Décor/Garden
67%	**71%**	**63%**	**71%**	**67%**	**63%**

Rejuvenated local with almost visibly designated areas for locals, traditional drinkers and modern arty pub afficionadoes. Lots of nice art with pool and darts for the hoi poloi. Food now widely regarded as exceptional.

Heart & Hand

56%
Pub Rating

Street: North Road
Area of Brighton: North Laine
Pub Type: Town & Local

Atmosphere	Beer	Barstaff	Food	Entertainment	Décor/Garden
60%	**52%**	**46%**	**46%**	**33%**	**38%**

Insular people, amazing jukebox and free food on a Sunday make for a unique pub experience. Wall full of information on Brighton's music scene from up to 30 years ago.

Hectors House

68%
Pub Rating

Street: Grand Parade
Area of Brighton: North Laine
Pub Type: Studenty

Atmosphere	Beer	Barstaff	Food	Entertainment	Décor/Garden
70%	**52%**	**48%**	**38%**	**55%**	**54%**

Large student drinking den. Recently done up from the previous apocalyptic decor, cheap drinks and rocking atmosphere (with loud music) late on. The red pool table is free during the day. DJs. Drinks promos.

Heist

39%
Pub Rating

Street: West Street
Area of Brighton: Clock Tower
Pub Type: Pre-club

Atmosphere	Beer	Barstaff	Food	Entertainment	Décor/Garden
25%	**42%**	**50%**	**33%**	**42%**	**42%**

A Black Gothic exterior doesn't give much clue to the inside. This place looks cool and relaxing while empty, but add the West Street horde and it is a lot different.....

Hobgoblin

81%
Pub Rating

Street: London Road/Cheapside
Area of Brighton: North Laine
Pub Type: Studenty & Town

Atmosphere	Beer	Barstaff	Food	Entertainment	Décor/Garden
77%	**59%**	**64%**	**43%**	**71%**	**57%**

Brighton's grungiest pub, but friendly and fun with live music some nights. Open till 1am on Friday and Saturday. Pop Pub Quiz on Monday.

Hole in the Wall

54%
Pub Rating

Street: Queensbury Mews
Area of Brighton: Western Road
Pub Type: Gay

Atmosphere	Beer	Barstaff	Food	Entertainment	Décor/Garden
46%	**50%**	**67%**	**27%**	**17%**	**65%**

Actually called the Queensbury Arms this used to be the smallest pub in Brighton, but isn't any more.....

Hollingbury Arms

55%
Pub Rating

Street: Hollingbury Rd
Area of Brighton: Ditchling Road
Pub Type: Local

Atmosphere	Beer	Barstaff	Food	Entertainment	Décor/Garden
42%	**50%**	**46%**	**33%**	**58%**	**58%**

Large local's pub. Very popular with sports fans.

Honey Club

59%
Pub Rating

Street: Kings Road Arches
Area of Brighton: Seafront
Pub Type: Pre-club

Atmosphere	Beer	Barstaff	Food	Entertainment	Décor/Garden
55%	**50%**	**45%**	**55%**	**50%**	**48%**

Bar on the beach thats really a big beat club later. Large outdoor seating area for watching the world go by.

Hop Poles

90%
Pub Rating

Street: Middle Street
Area of Brighton: Lanes
Pub Type: Town

Atmosphere	Beer	Barstaff	Food	Entertainment	Décor/Garden
79%	**67%**	**65%**	**77%**	**44%**	**92%**

Relaxed, modern pub with good beer, great food, music, garden, jars of sweets, friendly barstaff, modern art (hub-cap octopus on the roof and crocodile on the outside wall) and chilled music. Why aren't all modern pubs like this? Is often too full though.

Hope, The

46%
Pub Rating

Street: Queen's Road
Area of Brighton: Clock Tower
Pub Type: Town

Atmosphere	Beer	Barstaff	Food	Entertainment	Décor/Garden
41%	**38%**	**41%**	**34%**	**38%**	**59%**

Completely redecorated pubs which can't seem to keep the same name for a year [was "Desolate pub with cheap beer and bizarre entertainment upstairs"] which somehow seems almost exactly the same except for a nicer paint job and slightly nicer customers. Lots of new sofas are part of the new look.

Horatios

54%
Pub Rating

Street: The Pier
Area of Brighton: Seafront
Pub Type: Town

Atmosphere	Beer	Barstaff	Food	Entertainment	Décor/Garden
44%	**50%**	**38%**	**50%**	**75%**	**38%**

Vast hall of a bar with live music some nights and karaoke the others. Not recommended.

If you are a visitor to The Brighton Pier then you might find Horatios/The Offshore Bar/Victorias hard to resist

Horse & Groom

67%
Pub Rating

Street: Islingwood Road
Area of Brighton: Hanover
Pub Type: Local

Atmosphere	Beer	Barstaff	Food	Entertainment	Décor/Garden
59%	**53%**	**59%**	**25%**	**66%**	**53%**

Much-improved locals' pub up the road from the Unity. Some live music events.

Hotel du Vin

72%
Pub Rating

Street: Ship Street
Area of Brighton: Lanes
Pub Type: Town

Atmosphere	Beer	Barstaff	Food	Entertainment	Décor/Garden
75%	**25%**	**75%**	**75%**	**25%**	**88%**

Bar in a very fancy restaurant. Expensive and limited choice of drinks, but very nice surroundings and very expensive Cuban cigars on offer.

Hove Place

63%
Pub Rating

Street: First Avenue
Area of Brighton: Hove
Pub Type: Town

Atmosphere	Beer	Barstaff	Food	Entertainment	Décor/Garden
48%	**65%**	**46%**	**52%**	**42%**	**67%**

Deceptively spacious sunken pub with a large "Italian" beer garden; one of Hove's best-kept secrets. Rumoured to get rough some evenings - dubious clientele.

Hub, The

74%
Pub Rating

Street: The Gyratory
Area of Brighton: Ditchling Road
Pub Type: Local & Studenty

Atmosphere	Beer	Barstaff	Food	Entertainment	Décor/Garden
60%	**55%**	**60%**	**50%**	**60%**	**75%**

Table football, DJs, interesting furniture and expensive lager. Renamed from "No Man is an Island". You'll feel old if you are 30+.

I Go Inn

41%
Pub Rating

Street: Rock Street
Area of Brighton: Kemptown
Pub Type: Local

Atmosphere	Beer	Barstaff	Food	Entertainment	Décor/Garden
25%	**50%**	**50%**	**0%**	**56%**	**38%**

Should be called the "I go inn....and come straight back out again." Smokey, seedy, down-at-heel local. Dogs, children and old men welcome.

Iron Duke

57%
Pub Rating

Street: Waterloo St
Area of Brighton: Western Road
Pub Type: Gay

Atmosphere	Beer	Barstaff	Food	Entertainment	Décor/Garden
46%	**46%**	**54%**	**50%**	**58%**	**50%**

Refurbished pub/hotel. Comfortable, traditional decor and a relaxed atmosphere. Fair selection of drinks and food. Pool table, darts and gay-friendly.

Jolly Brewer

36%
Pub Rating

Street: Ditchling Road
Area of Brighton: Ditchling Road
Pub Type: Local

Atmosphere	Beer	Barstaff	Food	Entertainment	Décor/Garden
25%	**38%**	**33%**	**50%**	**58%**	**29%**

Tatty, unwelcoming local's pub. Abandon hope all ye who enter here.

Joogleberry Playhouse

70%
Pub Rating

Street: Manchester Street
Area of Brighton: St. James' Street
Pub Type: Town

Atmosphere	Beer	Barstaff	Food	Entertainment	Décor/Garden
63%	**38%**	**63%**	**50%**	**75%**	**63%**

Large café bar supporting the various entertainments of the playhouse. Draught lager on offer. Late bar with free entry.

Juggler

73%
Pub Rating

Street: Western Road
Area of Brighton: Western Road
Pub Type: Town

Atmosphere	Beer	Barstaff	Food	Entertainment	Décor/Garden
67%	**65%**	**69%**	**29%**	**50%**	**52%**

Chilled out bar with completely zombified upstairs. Friendly barstaff.

Jury's Out

42%
Pub Rating

Street: Edward Street
Area of Brighton: St. James' Street
Pub Type: Town

Atmosphere	Beer	Barstaff	Food	Entertainment	Décor/Garden
31%	**44%**	**50%**	**19%**	**38%**	**50%**

Renamed from the Thurlow Arms, but still an old-fashioned pub with atmosphere to match, but with nice new justice-style décor. Pool tables available. Live DJs at the weekend.

Katarina

49%
Pub Rating

Street: Marina
Area of Brighton: Kemptown
Pub Type: Town

Atmosphere	Beer	Barstaff	Food	Entertainment	Décor/Garden
38%	**50%**	**50%**	**59%**	**31%**	**50%**

Big Beefeater pub/restaurant overlooking a roundabout in the Marina. Little to recommend it over the other Marina choices.

King & Queen

63%
Pub Rating

Street: Malborough Place
Area of Brighton: North Laine
Pub Type: Town

Atmosphere	Beer	Barstaff	Food	Entertainment	Décor/Garden
50%	**54%**	**50%**	**43%**	**50%**	**71%**

Very big medieval pub with a room upstairs for parties. Robin Hood could swing off the chandeliers at any moment. You could wait ages to be served when its busy. Pool tables, table football and sky sports.

Kings Arms

53%
Pub Rating

Street: George Street
Area of Brighton: St. James' Street
Pub Type: Gay & Town

Atmosphere	Beer	Barstaff	Food	Entertainment	Décor/Garden
38%	**56%**	**50%**	**25%**	**50%**	**56%**

Spacious, comfortable and well-kept pub on the edge of Kemptown. Live music occasionally. Surprisingly dour customers covering a very mixed age group.

Koba

47%
Pub Rating

Street: Western Road
Area of Brighton: Western Road
Pub Type: Pre-club

Atmosphere	Beer	Barstaff	Food	Entertainment	Décor/Garden
50%	**25%**	**50%**	**0%**	**25%**	**75%**

A funky bar specialises in cocktails, Cuban fusion music and salubrious, velvety decor. Above Oddbins.

La Cachaca Bar

51%
Pub Rating

Street: Jubilee Street
Area of Brighton: North Laine
Pub Type: Town

Atmosphere	Beer	Barstaff	Food	Entertainment	Décor/Garden
50%	**25%**	**50%**	**50%**	**25%**	**75%**

Brazilian style bar connected to a restaurant with poor service. Expensive drinks, but nice cocktails.

La Tasca

54%
Pub Rating

Street: North Street
Area of Brighton: North Laine
Pub Type: Town

Atmosphere	Beer	Barstaff	Food	Entertainment	Décor/Garden
50%	**38%**	**50%**	**75%**	**25%**	**63%**

More of a restaurant than a spanish tapas bar, but you can have an expensive beer outside and some patatas bravas and pretend.

Le Lion D'Or

65%
Pub Rating

Street: George Street
Area of Brighton: Hove
Pub Type: Pre-club

Atmosphere	Beer	Barstaff	Food	Entertainment	Décor/Garden
63%	**38%**	**75%**	**0%**	**25%**	**88%**

Basically a wine bar. Fairly posh. Nothing on draught except Kronenbourg. Calls itself a "Wine Boutique", which is particularly posey!

Leconfield Arms

34%
Pub Rating

Street: Edward Street
Area of Brighton: St. James' Street
Pub Type: Local

Atmosphere	Beer	Barstaff	Food	Entertainment	Décor/Garden
25%	**38%**	**50%**	**38%**	**25%**	**38%**

Dreary brown pub. No doubt popular with its regulars, but nothing to recommend it.

Lectern

63%
Pub Rating

Street: Lewes Road
Area of Brighton: North Brighton
Pub Type: Studenty & Local

Atmosphere	Beer	Barstaff	Food	Entertainment	Décor/Garden
50%	**46%**	**42%**	**54%**	**67%**	**71%**

Spacious, refurbished studenty pub in downtown Lewes Road. Full of lager-drinking bright young things

Leek & Winkle

55%
Pub Rating

Street: Ditchling Road
Area of Brighton: Ditchling Road
Pub Type: Pre-club

Atmosphere	Beer	Barstaff	Food	Entertainment	Décor/Garden
48%	**52%**	**45%**	**43%**	**32%**	**63%**

Refurbished ex-pub; very smart but no longer has a heart. 'Amusements' area tucked away at the back

Leo's Lounge

28%
Pub Rating

Street: Meeting House Lane
Area of Brighton: Lanes
Pub Type: Pre-club

Atmosphere	Beer	Barstaff	Food	Entertainment	Décor/Garden
33%	**8%**	**17%**	**42%**	**21%**	**67%**

Outrageously expensive (£2.70 a pint) with only one draft beer available. Limited food. An up-market bar with smart decor, but so what?! Multiple leopardskin sofas for that lazy night. Renamed from the horrible Lanes End.

The Lion & Lobster used to be one of our favourite pubs.....

Lion and Lobster

78%
Pub Rating

Street: Bedford Square
Area of Brighton: Western Road
Pub Type: Studenty & Local

Atmosphere	Beer	Barstaff	Food	Entertainment	Décor/Garden
70%	**63%**	**64%**	**66%**	**54%**	**63%**

Really nice pub with good food and excellent decor, but sometimes dodgy beer

Lion and Unicorn

38%
Pub Rating

Street: Sussex St
Area of Brighton: Hanover
Pub Type: Local

Atmosphere	Beer	Barstaff	Food	Entertainment	Décor/Garden
38%	**38%**	**25%**	**0%**	**63%**	**31%**

Nicotine-stained locals' boozer. Loads of sports fans. Good jukebox

London to Brighton Hog

47%
Pub Rating

Street: London Road
Area of Brighton: Ditchling Road
Pub Type: Town

Atmosphere	Beer	Barstaff	Food	Entertainment	Décor/Garden
33%	**56%**	**38%**	**54%**	**33%**	**50%**

Good selection of beer but clueless barstaff and horrible customers

London Unity

72%
Pub Rating

Street: Islingwood Road
Area of Brighton: Hanover
Pub Type: Local

Atmosphere	Beer	Barstaff	Food	Entertainment	Décor/Garden
75%	**65%**	**50%**	**44%**	**38%**	**52%**

Regulars pub, unpredictably full or empty. Recently refurbished which lost some of the unique character. Darts and juke-box available.

Lord Nelson

57%
Pub Rating

Street: Trafalgar Street
Area of Brighton: North Laine
Pub Type: Town

Atmosphere	Beer	Barstaff	Food	Entertainment	Décor/Garden
43%	**58%**	**60%**	**58%**	**40%**	**48%**

Regulars mix with nearby office workers in standard but friendly surroundings. Popular, Albion, pre-match meeting point prior to trek to Withdean. Good Harveys available.

The Lord Nelson will serve you a good pint of Harveys

Stop Press: **Madeira, The** New plastic pub on seafront, draft score: **54%**

Malborough

67%
Pub Rating

Street: Princes Street
Area of Brighton: St. James' Street
Pub Type: Gay

Atmosphere	Beer	Barstaff	Food	Entertainment	Décor/Garden
63%	**53%**	**50%**	**44%**	**59%**	**56%**

Good atmosphere Lesbian pub with Theatre upstairs which shows a variety of unusual entertainment. Games night on a Wednesday from Jenga to Scrabble. Pub Quiz on a Sunday.

Marine Tavern

64%
Pub Rating

Street: Broad Street
Area of Brighton: St. James' Street
Pub Type: Gay & Local

Atmosphere	Beer	Barstaff	Food	Entertainment	Décor/Garden
56%	**56%**	**66%**	**25%**	**28%**	**72%**

Small but very well-kept locals' pub near the seafront. Feels more like a study than a pub. Wood panelling & leather, towels in the (marble) loos, chilled out, quiet, cosy with chandeliers. Now taken over by the guy behind the Hop Poles and Coopers Cask.

Market Inn

53%
Pub Rating

Street: Market Street
Area of Brighton: Lanes
Pub Type: Town

Atmosphere	Beer	Barstaff	Food	Entertainment	Décor/Garden
43%	**55%**	**50%**	**50%**	**35%**	**50%**

Wearisome, standard town centre pub with absolutely no memorable features with the exception of the hideously smelly toilets

Marquess of Exeter

61%
Pub Rating

Street: Upper Hamilton Rd
Area of Brighton: Seven Dials
Pub Type: Local

Atmosphere	Beer	Barstaff	Food	Entertainment	Décor/Garden
44%	**56%**	**44%**	**75%**	**63%**	**56%**

Elvis evenings, stars in their eyes, quizes, pool table & pinball machine make this blokes boozer with plastic plants a seriously different place

Martha Gunn

50%
Pub Rating

Street: Upper Lewes Road
Area of Brighton: Ditchling Road
Pub Type: Local

Atmosphere	Beer	Barstaff	Food	Entertainment	Décor/Garden
38%	**50%**	**50%**	**44%**	**59%**	**38%**

Noisy, but amiable locals' pub. Pool/Snooker tables are the prime focus, along with the telly and the Sunday roast.

Mash Tun

65%
Pub Rating

Street: Church Street
Area of Brighton: North Laine
Pub Type: Studenty & Pre-Club

Atmosphere	Beer	Barstaff	Food	Entertainment	Décor/Garden
59%	**46%**	**55%**	**57%**	**39%**	**68%**

Rainbow coloured, lively nightspot with no bitter. Jam-packed at the weekends with the pre-club crowd.

Definitely a good spot for a pavement beer while you watch the world go by

Master Mariner

64%
Pub Rating

Street: Marina
Area of Brighton: Kemptown
Pub Type: Town

Atmosphere	Beer	Barstaff	Food	Entertainment	Décor/Garden
54%	**54%**	**46%**	**63%**	**42%**	**71%**

Quite pleasant old-style pub in the Marina with all-wooden décor and wall-panelling. Seats outside look over the water and various yachts.

Medusa

58%
Pub Rating

Street: Preston Street
Area of Brighton: Western Road
Pub Type: Local

Atmosphere	Beer	Barstaff	Food	Entertainment	Décor/Garden
54%	**58%**	**54%**	**17%**	**38%**	**50%**

Bizarre wooden alley of a bar, which if not the smallest pub in Brighton is certainly the wierdest shaped. Was called Skid Row, no different

Mitre Tavern

27%
Pub Rating

Street: Baker Street
Area of Brighton: Ditchling Road
Pub Type: Local

Atmosphere	Beer	Barstaff	Food	Entertainment	Décor/Garden
10%	**48%**	**48%**	**30%**	**33%**	**25%**

Drab, complacent locals' pub" or "Slip back into the 1920s as you enter this king of dogs" or "Indifferent old codgers' boozer

Montpelier

41%
Pub Rating

Street: Upper North Street
Area of Brighton: Western Road
Pub Type: Local

Atmosphere	Beer	Barstaff	Food	Entertainment	Décor/Garden
28%	**44%**	**47%**	**38%**	**50%**	**34%**

Full of regulars and dogs. Somewhere you wish you hadn't gone in. Nice spicy crisps.

Montreal Arms

66%
Pub Rating

Street: Albion Hill
Area of Brighton: Hanover
Pub Type: Local

Atmosphere	Beer	Barstaff	Food	Entertainment	Décor/Garden
54%	**58%**	**46%**	**58%**	**67%**	**54%**

Above average 'local' with multiple bar games (darts, bar billiards, etc) available and theme food nights

It's a serious climb from the Lewes Road to the Montreal Arms, but worth the walk!

More

56%
Pub Rating

Street: Trafalgar Street
Area of Brighton: North Laine
Pub Type: Town

Atmosphere	Beer	Barstaff	Food	Entertainment	Décor/Garden
50%	**38%**	**50%**	**78%**	**25%**	**69%**

Tempting food, off-putting beer (expensive, no bitter), colourful decor and good sound system

Next door to the Mash Tun, Mrs Fitzherbert's is another good place for a pavement pint

Mrs Fitzherbert's

54%
Pub Rating

Street: New Road
Area of Brighton: North Laine
Pub Type: Town & Local

Atmosphere	Beer	Barstaff	Food	Entertainment	Décor/Garden
50%	**50%**	**50%**	**66%**	**25%**	**50%**

Small Luvvies hideout with self-congratulatory sign 'Best Pub Food in Brighton', though the menu looks well tasty, with seafood a speciality.

Neptune

54%
Pub Rating

Street: Victoria Terrace
Area of Brighton: Hove
Pub Type: Local

Atmosphere	Beer	Barstaff	Food	Entertainment	Décor/Garden
50%	**54%**	**46%**	**33%**	**42%**	**42%**

Sadly north-facing pub near Hove seafront. Olde-worlde with a certain charm and good beer. Not a patch on its Whitstable counterpart! Does serve Becks beer on draft.

Newmarket Arms

33%
Pub Rating

Street: Bear Road
Area of Brighton: Hanover
Pub Type: Local

Atmosphere	Beer	Barstaff	Food	Entertainment	Décor/Garden
19%	**38%**	**50%**	**25%**	**44%**	**38%**

Tired looking local boozer. Customers are not very lively. Darts available for those who have the energy to move their arms.

No Name Bar

61%
Pub Rating

Street: St. James' Street
Area of Brighton: St. James' Street
Pub Type: Town

Atmosphere	Beer	Barstaff	Food	Entertainment	Décor/Garden
50%	**50%**	**75%**	**75%**	**0%**	**75%**

Relaxed cocktail bar with a lot of class.

Northern Tavern

32%
Pub Rating

Street: Ditchling Road
Area of Brighton: Ditchling Road
Pub Type: Local

Atmosphere	Beer	Barstaff	Food	Entertainment	Décor/Garden
13%	**48%**	**40%**	**35%**	**58%**	**25%**

Refurbished but still-unwelcoming local boozer transplanted from an inner city danger area

Oak, The

75%
Pub Rating

Street: St. James' Street
Area of Brighton: St. James' Street
Pub Type: Local

Atmosphere	Beer	Barstaff	Food	Entertainment	Décor/Garden
63%	**63%**	**63%**	**50%**	**63%**	**63%**

Refurbished Kemptown pub (it needed it) now far more appealing and better than most of the other nearby pubs.

Office

55%
Pub Rating

Street: Sydney Street
Area of Brighton: North Laine
Pub Type: Town

Atmosphere	Beer	Barstaff	Food	Entertainment	Décor/Garden
50%	**52%**	**56%**	**67%**	**13%**	**54%**

Was "Soulless, angular, expensive and bleak" when it first opened, but has now worn in somewhat. Nice barstaff. Popular with new clientele. Really good lunchtime Thai food. Nice garden in the sun.

The Office garden is a good spot for food

Offshore Bar

59%
Pub Rating

Street: The Pier
Area of Brighton: Seafront
Pub Type: Town

Atmosphere	Beer	Barstaff	Food	Entertainment	Décor/Garden
63%	**25%**	**50%**	**25%**	**75%**	**50%**

Seemingly 24 hour karaoke bar can be crzay, but the best bet is just to go with it, or go.

Old Orleans

60%
Pub Rating

Street: Albert Street
Area of Brighton: Lanes
Pub Type: Town

Atmosphere	Beer	Barstaff	Food	Entertainment	Décor/Garden
48%	**70%**	**58%**	**60%**	**30%**	**45%**

Spacious bar with restaurant upstairs, recommended for the 'happy hour' cocktails. Newly refurbished means it has lost that certain something.

O'Neills

65%
Pub Rating

Street: Ship Street
Area of Brighton: Lanes
Pub Type: Irish & Town

Atmosphere	Beer	Barstaff	Food	Entertainment	Décor/Garden
63%	**64%**	**48%**	**50%**	**50%**	**39%**

Large Irish-style pub which is very lively on Fridays and Saturdays. occasional dancing in the back. Interesting little booths for hiding away in. Late night drinking available some nights.

O'Neill's is a good spot for some late night Guinness drinking

Open House

90%
Pub Rating

Street: Springfield Road
Area of Brighton: Ditchling Road
Pub Type: Local

Atmosphere	Beer	Barstaff	Food	Entertainment	Décor/Garden
90%	**50%**	**63%**	**58%**	**71%**	**79%**

Fairly new Zel-run pub/bar . Very arty decor and customers, in keeping with the thespian ambience of this part of Brighton. Good service, food, varied entertainment and a very large courtyard-come-beer garden which is fantastic in the summer.

The attractive bar (and barstaff!) in the excellent Open House

Oriental (The)

49%
Pub Rating

Street: Montpeliar Rd
Area of Brighton: Western Road
Pub Type: Gay

Atmosphere	Beer	Barstaff	Food	Entertainment	Décor/Garden
50%	**50%**	**56%**	**0%**	**25%**	**44%**

Well-kept gay pub with glitzy stage for wild live entertainment.

Palmeira

70%
Pub Rating

Street: Cromwell Road
Area of Brighton: Hove
Pub Type: Local

Atmosphere	Beer	Barstaff	Food	Entertainment	Décor/Garden
58%	**60%**	**55%**	**53%**	**60%**	**63%**

Big with no character and and on occaisions few customers, but nice barstaff. Sometimes popular with the locals. Jukebox.

Palmers Bar

61%
Pub Rating

Street: Queen's Square
Area of Brighton: Clock Tower
Pub Type: Town

Atmosphere	Beer	Barstaff	Food	Entertainment	Décor/Garden
63%	**44%**	**63%**	**38%**	**38%**	**50%**

Members only, but free to join. Great little place with good music (live DJs) and drinks specials

Park Crescent

74%
Pub Rating

Street: Park Crescent
Area of Brighton: Ditchling Road
Pub Type: Local

Atmosphere	Beer	Barstaff	Food	Entertainment	Décor/Garden
71%	**67%**	**58%**	**42%**	**42%**	**58%**

Popular large locals pub with a lively feel. Every seat is taken on a Friday and Saturday night. Good lagers, reasonable food and flighty bar-staff. The concrete yard out the back acts as a sort of beer garden.

Park View

76%
Pub Rating

Street: Preston Drove
Area of Brighton: North Brighton
Pub Type: Local

Atmosphere	Beer	Barstaff	Food	Entertainment	Décor/Garden
60%	**60%**	**60%**	**67%**	**63%**	**71%**

Recently refurbished large pub with a great quiz on a Tuesday and a big room downstairs for TV football

Pavillion Tavern

47%
Pub Rating

Street: North Street
Area of Brighton: Lanes
Pub Type: Pre-club

Atmosphere	Beer	Barstaff	Food	Entertainment	Décor/Garden
45%	**46%**	**32%**	**36%**	**48%**	**39%**

Sometimes unfriendly atmosphere but good if you are up for a clubby night out. Club upstairs with DJs every night.

Pedestrian Arms

49%
Pub Rating

Street: Foundry Street
Area of Brighton: North Laine
Pub Type: Local

Atmosphere	Beer	Barstaff	Food	Entertainment	Décor/Garden
34%	**50%**	**53%**	**28%**	**69%**	**31%**

Postmen's local with friendly barstaff, various entertainment. The inside has not seen daylight for several years.

The Pedestrian's Arms may be the single reason for the late delivery of your parcel

Plaza Bar

59%
Pub Rating

Street: Kings Road
Area of Brighton: Lanes
Pub Type: Town

Atmosphere	Beer	Barstaff	Food	Entertainment	Décor/Garden
38%	**50%**	**63%**	**63%**	**38%**	**75%**

Kings Road trying-but-failing to be posey Bar/Café. You just could be in so many better places round here. And not sat right on a busy road. Guys who look like the Brighton version of the Sopranos hang out here.

Polar (East)

39%
Pub Rating

Street: St George's Road
Area of Brighton: Kemptown
Pub Type: Pre-club

Atmosphere	Beer	Barstaff	Food	Entertainment	Décor/Garden
33%	**33%**	**33%**	**42%**	**42%**	**50%**

Previously the 'Burlington'. Now a smart but clinical and characterless young person's bar

Pond

58%
Pub Rating

Street: Gloucester Road
Area of Brighton: North Laine
Pub Type: Town

Atmosphere	Beer	Barstaff	Food	Entertainment	Décor/Garden
50%	**56%**	**50%**	**63%**	**33%**	**50%**

Cramped bar with postmen and a Thai restaurant upstairs which serves food in the evenings

The Pond in the North Laine will serve you a decent Thai meal upstairs

Portland Rock Bar

78%
Pub Rating

Street: Portland Road
Area of Brighton: Hove
Pub Type: Town

Atmosphere	Beer	Barstaff	Food	Entertainment	Décor/Garden
63%	**63%**	**50%**	**50%**	**88%**	**63%**

Actually beyond the boundaries set for this guide, but this is the only notable bar in western hove. Live rock music!

Pressure Point

68%
Pub Rating

Street: Grand Parade
Area of Brighton: Hanover
Pub Type: Studenty

Atmosphere	Beer	Barstaff	Food	Entertainment	Décor/Garden
57%	**61%**	**50%**	**59%**	**52%**	**59%**

Nice layout and decor but ignorant barstaff and unpredictable quality beer. Music can be extremely loud. With 'Caribbean Kitchen' at lunchtimes and some evenings.

Get your shouting head on if you are drinking in the Pressure Point

Preston Park Tavern

71%
Pub Rating

Street: Havelock Road
Area of Brighton: North Brighton
Pub Type: Local

Atmosphere	Beer	Barstaff	Food	Entertainment	Décor/Garden
63%	**65%**	**55%**	**50%**	**55%**	**55%**

Full of Albion supporters on a match night, big and L-shaped. Good for watching football and fights

Prestonville Arms

83%
Pub Rating

Street: Hamilton Road
Area of Brighton: Seven Dials
Pub Type: Town & Local

Atmosphere	Beer	Barstaff	Food	Entertainment	Décor/Garden
66%	**91%**	**56%**	**69%**	**44%**	**69%**

Sister pub to the Basketmakers with excellent Gales beer, top pub food and a good quiz. Comfortable surroundings. Bit of a boozers pub, due to beer quality.

Enjoy a superb pint in the Prestonville – if you can find it......

Prince Albert

68%
Pub Rating

Street: Trafalgar Street
Area of Brighton: North Laine
Pub Type: Town

Atmosphere	Beer	Barstaff	Food	Entertainment	Décor/Garden
55%	**65%**	**53%**	**50%**	**65%**	**50%**

Converted from a nightmare pub into quite a pleasant one. Big room upstairs for watching football. Cheap drink deals. Live Music, Flamenco evenings and tapas!

Prince Arthur

57%
Pub Rating

Street: Dean St
Area of Brighton: Western Road
Pub Type: Town

Atmosphere	Beer	Barstaff	Food	Entertainment	Décor/Garden
53%	**53%**	**53%**	**31%**	**25%**	**59%**

Small locals' boozer just off the Western Road. Could provide a reasonable escape from the horror of shopping

Prince of Wales

44%
Pub Rating

Street: Cannon Place
Area of Brighton: Clock Tower
Pub Type: Town

Atmosphere	Beer	Barstaff	Food	Entertainment	Décor/Garden
38%	**56%**	**41%**	**38%**	**19%**	**47%**

Cramped little pub, but provides handy escape from shopping hell

Prodigal

57%

Pub Rating

Street: East Street
Area of Brighton: Lanes
Pub Type: Pre-club

Atmosphere	Beer	Barstaff	Food	Entertainment	Décor/Garden
55%	**48%**	**39%**	**59%**	**36%**	**54%**

Very lively, strangely shaped, big pub on the edge of the Lanes, described by one juror as "sometimes full of wankers." Nice menu and views of the sea.

One juror describes the Prodigal, near the seafront, as a "Pub full of wankers"

Providence

45%

Pub Rating

Street: Western Road
Area of Brighton: Western Road
Pub Type: Town

Atmosphere	Beer	Barstaff	Food	Entertainment	Décor/Garden
42%	**46%**	**42%**	**46%**	**25%**	**46%**

Was the Bar Med, then the Litten Tree, which was "Bright and artificial but it does sell Becks on draught". Renamed but still exactly the same.

Pub With No Name

87%
Pub Rating

Street: Southover Street
Area of Brighton: Hanover
Pub Type: Pre-club & Local

Atmosphere	Beer	Barstaff	Food	Entertainment	Décor/Garden
78%	**70%**	**70%**	**58%**	**50%**	**75%**

This no-name pub is a warm, interesting, locals' pub like a house party with lots of rooms & friendly barstaff. It's well worth the climb up Southover Street. Good food, which you can usually see lots of people eating!

Pull & Pump

67%
Pub Rating

Street: Clarence Gardens
Area of Brighton: Western Road
Pub Type: Town & Local

Atmosphere	Beer	Barstaff	Food	Entertainment	Décor/Garden
63%	**52%**	**60%**	**42%**	**38%**	**65%**

Relaxed and friendly combination of locals and shoppers. Good selection of beers.

Pump House

58%
Pub Rating

Street: Market Street
Area of Brighton: Lanes
Pub Type: Town

Atmosphere	Beer	Barstaff	Food	Entertainment	Décor/Garden
46%	**63%**	**50%**	**54%**	**38%**	**50%**

From the outside, it looks like a cake shop. Inside it looks expensive and expansive yet is welcoming and comfortable. Can get lively.

PV (Princess Victoria)

66%
Pub Rating

Street: Church Street
Area of Brighton: Western Road
Pub Type: Town

Atmosphere	Beer	Barstaff	Food	Entertainment	Décor/Garden
66%	**56%**	**47%**	**31%**	**50%**	**56%**

Bit of a secretly nice pub hidden away here, it claims to have the friendliest barstaff in town. Happy hour promos 5-8pm.

Maybe not "the friendliest barstaff in town", but a decent place for a pint

Queens Arms

52%
Pub Rating

Street: George Street
Area of Brighton: St. James' Street
Pub Type: Gay

Atmosphere	Beer	Barstaff	Food	Entertainment	Décor/Garden
44%	**38%**	**50%**	**0%**	**63%**	**63%**

Long-established, lively, rather camp, totally gay, Kemptown pre-club bar. Quite good fun. Add live DJs and later on the whole place turns into a dance floor.

Queens Head (Steine)

67%
Pub Rating

Street: Steine Street
Area of Brighton: St. James' Street
Pub Type: Gay

Atmosphere	Beer	Barstaff	Food	Entertainment	Décor/Garden
67%	**46%**	**58%**	**33%**	**63%**	**50%**

Very mixed gay pub with drag shows - welcoming, laid back atmosphere

Queens Head (Stn)

42%
Pub Rating

Street: Queen's Road
Area of Brighton: North Laine
Pub Type: Town

Atmosphere	Beer	Barstaff	Food	Entertainment	Décor/Garden
31%	**44%**	**38%**	**44%**	**41%**	**47%**

Threatening atmosphere with a pool table and shiny decor

Racehill

40%
Pub Rating

Street: Lewes Road
Area of Brighton: Ditchling Road
Pub Type: Local

Atmosphere	Beer	Barstaff	Food	Entertainment	Décor/Garden
29%	**42%**	**46%**	**25%**	**63%**	**29%**

Slightly improved recently from "Sadly run-down and unwelcoming". Pool competitions

Racehorse

45%
Pub Rating

Street: Elm Grove
Area of Brighton: Hanover
Pub Type: Local

Atmosphere	Beer	Barstaff	Food	Entertainment	Décor/Garden
33%	**50%**	**38%**	**17%**	**58%**	**42%**

Spacious but drab, unwelcoming locals' pub, only 5 minutes' walk from superior competition

Railway Bell

40%
Pub Rating

Street: Surrey Street
Area of Brighton: Seven Dials
Pub Type: Local

Atmosphere	Beer	Barstaff	Food	Entertainment	Décor/Garden
13%	**46%**	**46%**	**8%**	**67%**	**58%**

Brighton's worst looking pub from the outside was finally refurbished and somehow turned into a worse pub! 'Tardis-like' in size, smokey locals' pub.

Railway Hotel

47%
Pub Rating

Street: Ditchling Rise
Area of Brighton: Ditchling Road
Pub Type: Local

Atmosphere	Beer	Barstaff	Food	Entertainment	Décor/Garden
33%	**46%**	**54%**	**33%**	**58%**	**38%**

Large and tatty locals' watering hole, in desperate need of a lick of paint. Proximity to London Road railway station is its only selling point. Recently changed ownership to zeroi effect.

The Ranelagh is a very decent pub in the middle of Kemptown

Ranelagh Arms

68%
Pub Rating

Street: High Street
Area of Brighton: St. James' Street
Pub Type: Local & Town

Atmosphere	Beer	Barstaff	Food	Entertainment	Décor/Garden
50%	**63%**	**63%**	**63%**	**56%**	**56%**

Really interesting Blues pub in the middle of Kemptown and close to the shops. Excellent musical decor and live Blues every Sunday. Can have a very lively 'local' atmosphere, maybe a bit smokey and loud. Good choice of food (steaks, curries and pub grub).

R-bar

36%
Pub Rating

Street: Marine Parade
Area of Brighton: Seafront
Pub Type: Pre-club

Atmosphere	Beer	Barstaff	Food	Entertainment	Décor/Garden
20%	**38%**	**40%**	**40%**	**45%**	**48%**

Renamed from Kruze which was renamed from Shooters. Not much change in this sea-front bar apart from it is now more gay than it was.

Red Lion

63%
Pub Rating

Street: Hove Place
Area of Brighton: Hove
Pub Type: Local

Atmosphere	Beer	Barstaff	Food	Entertainment	Décor/Garden
58%	**50%**	**50%**	**25%**	**58%**	**58%**

Backstreet Hove pub. Sky Sports a go-go!

Red Rum

71%
Pub Rating

Street: Western Road
Area of Brighton: Western Road
Pub Type: Town

Atmosphere	Beer	Barstaff	Food	Entertainment	Décor/Garden
63%	**50%**	**50%**	**75%**	**63%**	**63%**

Trendy new bar/restaurant serving tapas, "light bites" and burgers. Big flat screen TVs for sports events. Five draught beers on tap, plus bottles and a cocktail menu. Light and airy, but kind of lacking in soul. Cocktail happy hours some nights.

Redz

39%
Pub Rating

Street: Kings Road
Area of Brighton: Lanes
Pub Type: Town

Atmosphere	Beer	Barstaff	Food	Entertainment	Décor/Garden
25%	**25%**	**50%**	**50%**	**25%**	**75%**

Posey bar/brasserie right on the busy Kings Road. Your sanity needs testing if you are in here.

Regency

84%
Pub Rating

Street: Regency Mews
Area of Brighton: Western Road
Pub Type: Gay & Town

Atmosphere	Beer	Barstaff	Food	Entertainment	Décor/Garden
78%	**63%**	**70%**	**50%**	**45%**	**78%**

Another hard-to-find pub, it has possibly the most outrageous and ostentatious decor of any pub in Brighton. There is an interesting mix of punters and barstaff. Definitely gay-friendly, very camp and it features amazing disco toilets.

Reservoir

80%
Pub Rating

Street: Howard Road
Area of Brighton: Hanover
Pub Type: Town

Atmosphere	Beer	Barstaff	Food	Entertainment	Décor/Garden
75%	**69%**	**56%**	**69%**	**25%**	**81%**

Quite buzzy and trendy with a good choice of drinks, and proudly displays the slogan "May there be much boozing and sillyness (sic) ahead!" Amen to that, and certainly the place makes the nearby pubs look like the seedy old whores that they are

Riki Tik

54%
Pub Rating

Street: Bond Street
Area of Brighton: North Laine
Pub Type: Pre-club

Atmosphere	Beer	Barstaff	Food	Entertainment	Décor/Garden
58%	**35%**	**40%**	**48%**	**28%**	**65%**

Super trendy bar for clubbers. Cocktails are the drink to be supping.

Robin Hood

55%
Pub Rating

Street: Western Street
Area of Brighton: Western Road
Pub Type: Town

Atmosphere	Beer	Barstaff	Food	Entertainment	Décor/Garden
42%	**42%**	**42%**	**33%**	**58%**	**71%**

This "People's Pub" is a definate improvement on the 'Yobs pub' it used to be. All profits are donated to charity/the community and real Italian pizza is served. No bitters, but a good selection of draught lager.

Rock, The

80%
Pub Rating

Street: Rock Street
Area of Brighton: Kemptown
Pub Type: Local & Town

Atmosphere	Beer	Barstaff	Food	Entertainment	Décor/Garden
75%	**63%**	**56%**	**56%**	**69%**	**56%**

With pool tables, darts, table football and live music some nights, this is entertainment central. With an upstairs, back room, basement, beer garden and patio its also not short of options for seating. Pub Quiz on a Tuesday.

Rose Hill Tavern

67%
Pub Rating

Street: Rose Hill Terrace
Area of Brighton: Ditchling Road
Pub Type: Local

Atmosphere	Beer	Barstaff	Food	Entertainment	Décor/Garden
58%	**60%**	**50%**	**33%**	**58%**	**58%**

Strangely shaped local's pub with a friendly atmosphere and pool table

Roundhill

50%
Pub Rating

Street: Ditchling Road
Area of Brighton: Ditchling Road
Pub Type: Local

Atmosphere	Beer	Barstaff	Food	Entertainment	Décor/Garden
33%	**48%**	**50%**	**45%**	**63%**	**48%**

Down to Earth, friendly locals' pub; regular Sky sports, Pool table and pub grub; can be too noisy. Quiz and live music nights. Frequently runs out of real ale.

Royal Sovereign

65%
Pub Rating

Street: Preston Street
Area of Brighton: Western Road
Pub Type: Town

Atmosphere	Beer	Barstaff	Food	Entertainment	Décor/Garden
50%	**63%**	**56%**	**53%**	**56%**	**53%**

Good all-round town centre pub, with beer garden. Ideally located for a pre or post dinner drink in one of the many eateries on this street.

Royal Standard

30%
Pub Rating

Street: Queen's Road
Area of Brighton: North Laine
Pub Type: Town & Local

Atmosphere	Beer	Barstaff	Food	Entertainment	Décor/Garden
25%	31%	50%	31%	25%	31%

Intimate little pub in the no man's land between the station and town. Can be very quiet/dull depending on your viewpoint.

Saint, The

48%
Pub Rating

Street: St. James' Street
Area of Brighton: St. James' Street
Pub Type: Gay

Atmosphere	Beer	Barstaff	Food	Entertainment	Décor/Garden
38%	38%	63%	75%	13%	63%

Subtley gay pub which considers beer to be Stella and Hoegarden

Salsa Bar

28%
Pub Rating

Street: Middle Street
Area of Brighton: Lanes
Pub Type: Local

Atmosphere	Beer	Barstaff	Food	Entertainment	Décor/Garden
13%	42%	42%	33%	33%	33%

Dreary town centre bar with the red lighting making is a good contender for 'The Pub from Hell', easily outclassed by more alert and awake competitors. Smelly toilets - always a bad sign!

Sanctuary Café

63%
Pub Rating

Street: Brunswick Street East
Area of Brighton: Western Road
Pub Type: Local

Atmosphere	Beer	Barstaff	Food	Entertainment	Décor/Garden
60%	40%	55%	80%	40%	58%

Funky café that also serves beer. Small bar downstairs. Entertainment often and unpredictable. Sometimes extended hours.

Santa Fe

63%
Pub Rating

Street: East Street
Area of Brighton: Lanes
Pub Type: Cocktail

Atmosphere	Beer	Barstaff	Food	Entertainment	Décor/Garden
63%	**38%**	**75%**	**50%**	**25%**	**63%**

Barstaff throwing bottles around like demented Tom Cruises in Cocktail, just make sure you are there in happy hour because otherwise it is just overpriced so-so cocktails. Nice selection of Mexican beer though. No beer on draft.

Saqqarra

67%
Pub Rating

Street: North Street
Area of Brighton: North Laine
Pub Type: Cocktail

Atmosphere	Beer	Barstaff	Food	Entertainment	Décor/Garden
75%	**38%**	**50%**	**50%**	**25%**	**75%**

Large fancy cocktail bar in vaguely eqyptian style. Expensive drinks, but try the one with fresh raspberry puree - amazing!

Seafield, The

38%
Pub Rating

Street: Church Road
Area of Brighton: Hove
Pub Type: Local

Atmosphere	Beer	Barstaff	Food	Entertainment	Décor/Garden
25%	**50%**	**50%**	**25%**	**25%**	**44%**

Smokey, unwelcoming, gloomy Church Road pub with live horse-racing on the telly. Does that say it all?

Seagull, The

33%
Pub Rating

Street: Madiera Drive
Area of Brighton: Seafront
Pub Type: Town

Atmosphere	Beer	Barstaff	Food	Entertainment	Décor/Garden
25%	**38%**	**50%**	**50%**	**0%**	**50%**

Bar/café/chippy with only the cold lager it serves as a good point. Take the beer and sit on the beach.

Setting Sun, The

53%
Pub Rating

Street: Windmill Street
Area of Brighton: Hanover
Pub Type: Local

Atmosphere	Beer	Barstaff	Food	Entertainment	Décor/Garden
50%	**38%**	**29%**	**38%**	**33%**	**83%**

Was The Miller's Arms, a "Dubious locals' pub". Now refurbished by the Full Moon Crew. Still with the same spectacular views. Due to have "Jukebox and Piano Shenanigans". Pub Quiz on a Tuesday. Very eco-friendly pub!

Sunset view from the Setting Sun pub garden

Shakespeare's Head (Spring St)

57%
Pub Rating

Street: Spring Street
Area of Brighton: Western Road
Pub Type: Town

Atmosphere	Beer	Barstaff	Food	Entertainment	Décor/Garden
47%	**50%**	**47%**	**50%**	**50%**	**56%**

Clean and spacious pub behind the Western Road. Lots of sports fans: a bit of a lads pub. Not enough barstaff, too many teenagers.

Shakespeare's Head (stn)

80%
Pub Rating

Street: Chatham Place
Area of Brighton: Seven Dials
Pub Type: Studenty

Atmosphere	Beer	Barstaff	Food	Entertainment	Décor/Garden
70%	**68%**	**70%**	**43%**	**54%**	**64%**

ZEL pub with barstaff who bring drinks to your table and a good selection of expensive lager. Alledgedly Kylie Minogue drank here! Pub Quiz on a Monday.

The Shakespeare's Head, behind Brighton Station, is an excellent pub

Sidewinder

84%
Pub Rating

Street: St. James' Street
Area of Brighton: St. James' Street
Pub Type: Town

Atmosphere	Beer	Barstaff	Food	Entertainment	Décor/Garden
78%	**55%**	**60%**	**55%**	**60%**	**85%**

You can spot this one by the disturbing crab/eye painting on the outside. This medium sized bar is always packed and no wonder given the great music, comfy seats and modern art decor. A good selection of beers on draught, a large beer garden and some interesting games round it off nicely.

The Sidewinder is a lot more welcoming than its disturbing outside would lead you to expect!

Slug & Lettuce

49%
Pub Rating

Street: George Street
Area of Brighton: Hove
Pub Type: Town

Atmosphere	Beer	Barstaff	Food	Entertainment	Décor/Garden
50%	**38%**	**38%**	**75%**	**13%**	**63%**

Disappointing. Flashy, vulgar, trashy, with an unimpressive range of beers. Basically a Hogshead wannabe - and that's not a recommendation!

Smugglers Arms

73%
Pub Rating

Street: Ship Street
Area of Brighton: Lanes
Pub Type: Studenty & Pre-Club

Atmosphere	Beer	Barstaff	Food	Entertainment	Décor/Garden
57%	**54%**	**50%**	**46%**	**79%**	**75%**

Supposedly good for lunch, dead before 8pm and packed after 9pm.
This place was finally refurbished after 25 years and is now a classy bar with an upmarket burger menu and has many more pool tables than previously.

Snafu 23

66%
Pub Rating

Street: Church Road
Area of Brighton: Hove
Pub Type: Pre-club

Atmosphere	Beer	Barstaff	Food	Entertainment	Décor/Garden
75%	**38%**	**38%**	**44%**	**38%**	**75%**

Totally revamped from the funky "Bar Zen". Now a wine bar with excellent food.
Turns into a club later.

The 'Sir Charles Napier' – see "Charles Napier in the A-Z, bit of a snafu….

Sportsman

44%
Pub Rating

Street: London Road
Area of Brighton: North Brighton
Pub Type: Local

Atmosphere	Beer	Barstaff	Food	Entertainment	Décor/Garden
25%	**50%**	**75%**	**25%**	**25%**	**50%**

A cavernous pub/restaurant, with a mock ancestral home theme (for some obscure reason), located next to the Withdean Sports Stadium and Sports Centre. Ideal for Brighton & Hove Albion FC fans, it also caters for families and children, including a large indoor play area. Not frequented by a great number of Locals and the majority of adult customers seem to pop in for an orange juice and lemonade after a game of squash next door.

Spread Eagle

43%
Pub Rating

Street: Albion Hill
Area of Brighton: Hanover
Pub Type: Local

Atmosphere	Beer	Barstaff	Food	Entertainment	Décor/Garden
31%	**47%**	**50%**	**38%**	**41%**	**38%**

Down to Earth local where Gary Sparrow might hang out. Cluttered with loads of trophies and other crap. Dubious disco at the weekend.

St. Christophers Inn

68%
Pub Rating

Street: Kings Road
Area of Brighton: Seafront
Pub Type: Town

Atmosphere	Beer	Barstaff	Food	Entertainment	Décor/Garden
63%	**56%**	**50%**	**50%**	**63%**	**50%**

Large middle-of-the-road bar, somehow hidden away right on the Kings Road

St. James Tavern

71%
Pub Rating

Street: St. James' Street
Area of Brighton: St. James' Street
Pub Type: Town

Atmosphere	Beer	Barstaff	Food	Entertainment	Décor/Garden
72%	**47%**	**50%**	**50%**	**47%**	**69%**

Pleasant decor and chilled out/happening atmosphere with occasional DJs playing 'Pre-Club Sounds'. Live Jazz on the last Sunday of the month. Dodgy toilet facilities. Very nice Thai food on offer.

The Saint James also serves some very nice Thai food

Stag

71%
Pub Rating

Street: Upper Bedford Street
Area of Brighton: St. James' Street
Pub Type: Local & Town

Atmosphere	Beer	Barstaff	Food	Entertainment	Décor/Garden
67%	**50%**	**50%**	**50%**	**67%**	**58%**

Well-kept and deceptively spacious Kemptown pub. Good selection of food and entertainment 3 evenings per week (e.g. 60s/70s cover band on Fridays)

The Stag in Kemptown is a good traditional pub

Standard, The

67%
Pub Rating

Street: West Street
Area of Brighton: Clock Tower
Pub Type: Town

Atmosphere	Beer	Barstaff	Food	Entertainment	Décor/Garden
56%	**50%**	**50%**	**63%**	**56%**	**69%**

The new, modern, acceptable face of West Street. Large, clean and well designed pub with a bright, airy beer garden.

Stanmer Park

50%
Pub Rating

Street: Ditchling Road
Area of Brighton: North Brighton
Pub Type: Local

Atmosphere	Beer	Barstaff	Food	Entertainment	Décor/Garden
31%	**50%**	**44%**	**50%**	**56%**	**56%**

Large, regularly re-decorated pub, probably due to damage from brawls. Shouting at Sky Sports is a favourite pastime here.

Star Inn, The

60%
Pub Rating

Street: Manchester Street
Area of Brighton: St. James' Street
Pub Type: Town

Atmosphere	Beer	Barstaff	Food	Entertainment	Décor/Garden
50%	**63%**	**50%**	**33%**	**42%**	**54%**

Boringly average town pub on the edge of Kemptown, with a wide selection of drinks, locks on the toilets, recently converted from the Golden Lion

Station, The (Hove)

60%
Pub Rating

Street: Goldstone Villas (next to Hove Station)
Area of Brighton: Hove
Pub Type: Town & Local

Atmosphere	Beer	Barstaff	Food	Entertainment	Décor/Garden
53%	**44%**	**44%**	**66%**	**50%**	**63%**

Extensively and expensively refurbished pub next to Hove station. Good choice of food. Lively atmosphere. The pub's new name no longer qualifies for inclusion in the Guinness Book of Records.

Station, The (Preston Park)

59%
Pub Rating

Street: Woodside Avenue
Area of Brighton: North Brighton
Pub Type: Town

Atmosphere	Beer	Barstaff	Food	Entertainment	Décor/Garden
63%	**50%**	**75%**	**0%**	**38%**	**38%**

Courage pub next to Preston Park station. Slightly sports orientated and rather drab, but welcoming. Okay in moderate doses.

Stirling Arms

53%
Pub Rating

Street: Stirling Place
Area of Brighton: Hove
Pub Type: Local

Atmosphere	Beer	Barstaff	Food	Entertainment	Décor/Garden
44%	**56%**	**50%**	**25%**	**56%**	**38%**

Traditional but quite decent locals' boozer in the back streets of Hove. Reasonable range of drinks, plus pool table, music and slot machines.

Strada

41%
Pub Rating

Street: North Street
Area of Brighton: North Laine
Pub Type: Town

Atmosphere	Beer	Barstaff	Food	Entertainment	Décor/Garden
25%	**25%**	**75%**	**75%**	**0%**	**75%**

Classy and relaxed bar and restaurant. Very expensive and only the bar section only just qualifies as a bar for this list. Little change from when it was called "Quod".

Sudeley Arms

40%
Pub Rating

Street: Sudeley St
Area of Brighton: Kemptown
Pub Type: Local

Atmosphere	Beer	Barstaff	Food	Entertainment	Décor/Garden
25%	**50%**	**38%**	**50%**	**44%**	**38%**

Very much a locals' pub: street corner, slightly shabby but popular with its regulars. Some reasonably-priced food. Ancient Teddy Boy with a turntable rocks the joint on Fridays!

Suga Qube

57%
Pub Rating

Street: North Street
Area of Brighton: Lanes
Pub Type: Town

Atmosphere	Beer	Barstaff	Food	Entertainment	Décor/Garden
50%	**56%**	**56%**	**13%**	**31%**	**63%**

The North Street bar changed yet again from the Altar Bar. It remains as a cool-looking bar in an unfortunate location. Open deck turntables are the only thing to distinguish it.

Sumo

44%
Pub Rating

Street: Middle Street
Area of Brighton: Lanes
Pub Type: Pre-club

Atmosphere	Beer	Barstaff	Food	Entertainment	Décor/Garden
29%	**25%**	**50%**	**50%**	**42%**	**75%**

Swanky bar which turns into a hellishly packed small nightclub (downstairs) later. Late licence. Club gone wrong.

Sussex (Btn Lanes)

60%
Pub Rating

Street: East Street
Area of Brighton: Lanes
Pub Type: Town

Atmosphere	Beer	Barstaff	Food	Entertainment	Décor/Garden
48%	**53%**	**55%**	**68%**	**50%**	**50%**

Relaxed, busy town centre pub. Can be packed and smokey.

Sussex (Hove Seafront)

70%
Pub Rating

Street: Victoria Terrace
Area of Brighton: Hove
Pub Type: Town

Atmosphere	Beer	Barstaff	Food	Entertainment	Décor/Garden
58%	**58%**	**53%**	**63%**	**60%**	**65%**

Very large seafront pub in Kingsway, Hove. Wide-ranging clientele and a reasonable range of drinks and food. The beer garden has a fountain!

Sussex Cricketers

62%
Pub Rating

Street: Eaton Road
Area of Brighton: Hove
Pub Type: Local

Atmosphere	Beer	Barstaff	Food	Entertainment	Décor/Garden
50%	**56%**	**44%**	**46%**	**50%**	**67%**

Big pub with lots of cricketers and nicotine. Right next to the cricket ground. A bit like drinking in a big hotel's bar.

The Sussex (in the Lanes) and Sussex Yeoman (near the Station)

Sussex Yeoman

63%
Pub Rating

Street: Guildford Rd
Area of Brighton: Seven Dials
Pub Type: Town & Studenty

Atmosphere	Beer	Barstaff	Food	Entertainment	Décor/Garden
53%	**58%**	**45%**	**60%**	**38%**	**68%**

Amazing colours and boardgames to play. Good food in large portions. Pub Quiz on a Tuesday.

Sutherland Arms

38%
Pub Rating

Street: Sutherland Rd
Area of Brighton: Kemptown
Pub Type: Local

Atmosphere	Beer	Barstaff	Food	Entertainment	Décor/Garden
25%	**38%**	**25%**	**50%**	**50%**	**50%**

Smokey, unwelcoming local's pub

Temple Bar

57%
Pub Rating

Street: Western Road
Area of Brighton: Western Road
Pub Type: Local

Atmosphere	Beer	Barstaff	Food	Entertainment	Décor/Garden
45%	**48%**	**50%**	**53%**	**58%**	**55%**

Multiple changes of management during 2005/6 has radically changed this pub. Its used to be "for regulars and hard bastards only", but now this football pub is quite nice, with friendly barstaff and an upstairs pool room. Big screens for football/sports.

The Temple Bar is distinctly unlike its namesake in Dublin

Terraces

40%
Pub Rating

Street: Marine Parade
Area of Brighton: Seafront
Pub Type: Town

Atmosphere	Beer	Barstaff	Food	Entertainment	Décor/Garden
38%	**25%**	**25%**	**38%**	**25%**	**75%**

Over-priced drinks, not much choice, rude barstaff, mediocre food. Methinks this place is relying on its amazing location.

Three Jolly Butchers (3jb)

65%
Pub Rating

Street: North Road
Area of Brighton: North Laine
Pub Type: Local

Atmosphere	Beer	Barstaff	Food	Entertainment	Décor/Garden
58%	**54%**	**54%**	**54%**	**33%**	**67%**

Re-named the terribly trendy "3jb" its an improvement from the "Cramped and not very jolly" place that it was, but the prices seem to have shot up to pay for the new décor.....

Good sandwiches and expensive beer are the main features of the 3jb

Tin Drum (5 ways)

49%
Pub Rating

Street: Ditchling Road
Area of Brighton: North Brighton
Pub Type: Town

Atmosphere	Beer	Barstaff	Food	Entertainment	Décor/Garden
47%	**34%**	**53%**	**50%**	**22%**	**59%**

Fourth after supposedly 'final' third member of the Tin Drum family in Brighton. Good food, comfortable but predictable.

Tin Drum (Hove)

67%
Pub Rating

Street: 2nd Avenue
Area of Brighton: Hove
Pub Type: Town

Atmosphere	Beer	Barstaff	Food	Entertainment	Décor/Garden
63%	50%	50%	75%	25%	75%

Third and supposedly final member of the Tin Drum family in Brighton. Good food, comfortable but predictable.

Tin Drum (Seven Dials)

50%
Pub Rating

Street: Dyke Road
Area of Brighton: Seven Dials
Pub Type: Town

Atmosphere	Beer	Barstaff	Food	Entertainment	Décor/Garden
45%	35%	55%	63%	25%	60%

Fabulous, dahling! Large, trendy Seven Dials bar with good choice of foods. Interesting range of drinks, but no real beer.

Tin Drum (St James' St)

50%
Pub Rating

Street: St. James' Street
Area of Brighton: St. James' Street
Pub Type: Town

Atmosphere	Beer	Barstaff	Food	Entertainment	Décor/Garden
38%	42%	63%	63%	25%	58%

Smart, clean,comfortable, Kemptown bar/restaurant. 2nd in the trilogy

Tzar Bar

59%
Pub Rating

Street:	Kings Road Arches
Area of Brighton:	Seafront
Pub Type:	Pre-club

Atmosphere	Beer	Barstaff	Food	Entertainment	Décor/Garden
50%	**25%**	**38%**	**50%**	**63%**	**88%**

Seafront bar with high quality modern decor and music videos playing inside. Waitress service in the appealling blue compound on the beach, with director-type chairs that look more comfortable than they are. Drinks expensive and limited range

Vavoom

46%
Pub Rating

Street:	The Steine
Area of Brighton:	St. James' Street
Pub Type:	Gay

Atmosphere	Beer	Barstaff	Food	Entertainment	Décor/Garden
38%	**50%**	**50%**	**0%**	**25%**	**63%**

New gay bar opened next to the Revenge club

Victoria, The

65%
Pub Rating

Street: Richmond Road
Area of Brighton: Ditchling Road
Pub Type: Local

Atmosphere	Beer	Barstaff	Food	Entertainment	Décor/Garden
55%	**55%**	**48%**	**35%**	**58%**	**65%**

Refurbished local boozer. Now a relaxed, comfortable, arty pub with drinks deals & beer garden. Nice buzz of conversation, quiz on a Tuesday, pool table.

Fancy a scone with your pint?

Victoria's Bar

70%
Pub Rating

Street: The Pier
Area of Brighton: Seafront
Pub Type: Town

Atmosphere	Beer	Barstaff	Food	Entertainment	Décor/Garden
69%	**38%**	**56%**	**56%**	**50%**	**75%**

Quaint pub on the pier is a lot better than you'd expect. Food is chips with everything……or tea and scones!

Victory Inn

57%
Pub Rating

Street: Duke Street
Area of Brighton: Lanes
Pub Type: Town & Local

Atmosphere	Beer	Barstaff	Food	Entertainment	Décor/Garden
50%	**56%**	**50%**	**53%**	**25%**	**59%**

So-so town centre pub transported through time from 1962 - now refurbished and upto 1985. Comfy sofas.

The Victory has a small bar, but a lounge stuffed with sofas!

Volks Bar

61%
Pub Rating

Street: Madiera Drive
Area of Brighton: Seafront
Pub Type: Pre-club & Town

Atmosphere	Beer	Barstaff	Food	Entertainment	Décor/Garden
50%	**50%**	**63%**	**50%**	**25%**	**75%**

Just over the dangerous boy racer Madeira Drive from the beach, Volks has decided to cash in the on increasing popularity of the beach to the left of the pier by opening during the day as a bar as well as a club at night. Little to drag you here but convenience though.....

Waggon & Horses

66%
Pub Rating

Street: Church Street
Area of Brighton: North Laine
Pub Type: Town

Atmosphere	Beer	Barstaff	Food	Entertainment	Décor/Garden
65%	**65%**	**63%**	**50%**	**25%**	**46%**

Friendly atmosphere with lively barstaff and innumerable whiskies on offer

Great for a pint in the sun in the summer, or a pint and a whisky in the winter

Walkabout

69%
Pub Rating

Street: West Street
Area of Brighton: Clock Tower
Pub Type: Town & Pre-Club

Atmosphere	Beer	Barstaff	Food	Entertainment	Décor/Garden
63%	**42%**	**42%**	**67%**	**83%**	**58%**

Large Australasian sports bar, enough said.

Walmer, The

83%
Pub Rating

Street: Queen's Park Road
Area of Brighton: Hanover
Pub Type: Local

Atmosphere	Beer	Barstaff	Food	Entertainment	Décor/Garden
70%	**68%**	**55%**	**65%**	**65%**	**75%**

Wild colours and fish tanks with a good quiz. Good local colour and friendly atmosphere.

According to the jury, The Walmer is the 9th best pub in Brighton

Waves

30%
Pub Rating

Street: Madiera Drive
Area of Brighton: Seafront
Pub Type: Town

Atmosphere	Beer	Barstaff	Food	Entertainment	Décor/Garden
25%	**38%**	**50%**	**50%**	**0%**	**38%**

Bar/café/chippy with only the cold lager it serves as a good point. Take the beer and sit on the beach.

Wellington (Elm Grove)

37%
Pub Rating

Street: Elm Grove
Area of Brighton: Hanover
Pub Type: Local

Atmosphere	Beer	Barstaff	Food	Entertainment	Décor/Garden
29%	**42%**	**38%**	**17%**	**42%**	**42%**

Clean but rowdy local's pub

Wellington (Kemptown)

82%
Pub Rating

Street: College Place
Area of Brighton: Kemptown
Pub Type: Local

Atmosphere	Beer	Barstaff	Food	Entertainment	Décor/Garden
75%	**63%**	**63%**	**50%**	**63%**	**69%**

A traditional, busy Kemptown pub, the "Wellie" (so-called) has efficient barstaff, reasonable beer and a friendly atmosphere. Fairly spacious - you should be able to find a table if you want one. Raises lots of money for charity.

In the battle of the Wellingtons there is a clear winner......

West Quay

55%
Pub Rating

Street: Marina
Area of Brighton: Kemptown
Pub Type: Town

Atmosphere	Beer	Barstaff	Food	Entertainment	Décor/Garden
38%	**50%**	**44%**	**50%**	**44%**	**75%**

Huge pub/restaurant in the guise of a brick monstrosity on the sea-side of the Marina. Lovely views out to sea.

The Western Front features 2 floors – chilled out upstairs and loud as hell downstairs

Western Front

62%
Pub Rating

Street: Cranbourne St
Area of Brighton: Clock Tower
Pub Type: Studenty & Town

Atmosphere	Beer	Barstaff	Food	Entertainment	Décor/Garden
56%	**54%**	**58%**	**46%**	**29%**	**63%**

Good for a chill-out drink after escaping from Churchill Square shopping hell

White Horse

53%
Pub Rating

Street: Camelford Street
Area of Brighton: St. James' Street
Pub Type: Local

Atmosphere	Beer	Barstaff	Food	Entertainment	Décor/Garden
50%	**50%**	**50%**	**25%**	**44%**	**44%**

Relaxed, professional but dingy gay pub

William IV

42%
Pub Rating

Street: Church Street
Area of Brighton: North Laine
Pub Type: Town

Atmosphere	Beer	Barstaff	Food	Entertainment	Décor/Garden
38%	**45%**	**53%**	**50%**	**23%**	**33%**

Complacent, uninspiring pub that relies on its excellent location

One day the William the Fourth will live up to its potential

Windmill

70%
Pub Rating

Street: Upper North Street
Area of Brighton: Western Road
Pub Type: Town

Atmosphere	Beer	Barstaff	Food	Entertainment	Décor/Garden
60%	**60%**	**56%**	**58%**	**40%**	**67%**

Totally refurbished. Smart, lively and well-run, although a lot of the old informal atmosphere has been lost [Low beamed darts pub thats a good place for a chat]

The Windmill has transformed itself and is a lot more popular as a result

Winner

60%
Pub Rating

Street: Elm Grove
Area of Brighton: Hanover
Pub Type: Local

Atmosphere	Beer	Barstaff	Food	Entertainment	Décor/Garden
56%	**38%**	**56%**	**0%**	**75%**	**56%**

Bright, friendly pub next to Brighton Race Course. Worth popping in for a relaxed drink if you're in the area. Darts, pool, fruities, sport & racing on the telly provide the entertainment in this traditional working man's local, with occasional live music, too.

wwwater.bar

39%
Pub Rating

Street: Town Hall Square
Area of Brighton: Lanes
Pub Type: Town

Atmosphere	Beer	Barstaff	Food	Entertainment	Décor/Garden
25%	**38%**	**50%**	**0%**	**25%**	**75%**

Bar hiding at the bottom of the Thistle hotel in the square at the southern end of the Lanes. Lots of modern square furniture and a lack of atmosphere.

Yates'

46%
Pub Rating

Street: West Street
Area of Brighton: Clock Tower
Pub Type: Pre-Club & Town

Atmosphere	Beer	Barstaff	Food	Entertainment	Décor/Garden
38%	**47%**	**38%**	**44%**	**38%**	**50%**

Like Yates' everywhere. Noisy, garish and full after 9pm. Typical West Steet pub.

Zone Bar

34%
Pub Rating

Street: West Street
Area of Brighton: Clock Tower
Pub Type: Pre-club

Atmosphere	Beer	Barstaff	Food	Entertainment	Décor/Garden
25%	**31%**	**44%**	**50%**	**25%**	**50%**

Completely changed from the Margaritas Café/Bar into a full on Pre-club joint

Zone, The

44%
Pub Rating

Street: St. James' Street
Area of Brighton: St. James' Street
Pub Type: Gay

Atmosphere	Beer	Barstaff	Food	Entertainment	Décor/Garden
25%	**38%**	**50%**	**0%**	**63%**	**63%**

Now redecorated into a rather gay 'piano' bar with particularly fetching pink fluffy curtains.

Zoot Street

68%
Pub Rating

Street: Queens Road
Area of Brighton: Clock Tower
Pub Type: Town

Atmosphere	Beer	Barstaff	Food	Entertainment	Décor/Garden
63%	**50%**	**69%**	**0%**	**50%**	**69%**

Boasts "Cocktails, Blues, Jazz" and replaces the unpopular "Cord". Live music on some weekdays. The only pub in Brighton that plays exclusively blues and jazz music. Little choice of beer.

THE FUN

Pub Crawls

Here are a few ideas for pub crawls which will take you around both the more and less popular parts of town. Each one takes in about ten pubs, so if you want to remember any of the later pubs then half pints are recommended in some or all of them! If you can complete this little lot then you will have seen almost all of the best pubs in town and be well on the way to being a potential pub juror yourself, so take along a pad and pen and get scoring!

The Seafront Run

This actually requires no instructions at all. Simply start at either the Brighton (Palace!) Pier or the (derelict) West Pier and stroll along, stopping for drinks as you go. Actually, lets give you a bit more detail than that. Start for a very quick one in the Bar de la Mer near the ruins of the West Pier then walk toward the Palace Pier and stop at Gemini on the ellipse where you may well be treated to some live music. If you can drag yourself away from there then the next stop will be the Fortunes of War before moving on to Arc and/or Club Barracuda to get a beer that you can take onto the beach. Assuming you still feel like moving then you can make your way onto a bit more structured drinking and maybe a snack outside the Beach or Honey Club. Staggering onwards, have an expensive pint in the sun at the Tzar Bar. By this point you will probably not be in an acceptable state to be admitted to the Boardwalk and might not have the patience to wait for the service there, so move onto the Pier for a beer and some candyfloss in Victoria's bar and finally onto the log flume before throwing yourself into the karaoke nightmare of Horatios or the Offshore Bar! Good luck with that first verse of 'My Way'.

The Circuit Touristique

Starting at the Brighton station, this route will take you around the sights of Brighton's centre, with your weary limbs lubricated sufficiently by alcohol. If you get lost you can follow the circular metal bird signs on the pavement and lampposts to get you back to familiar territory.
Go straight out of the station and into the surprisingly pleasant Grand Central for your opening salvo. Out from there and down the underpass onto Trafalgar Street to the traditional Nelson for an excellent pint of Harveys, the local beer. Continue down Trafalgar Street until you reach Sydney Street. Steel yourself against being tempted into the array of interesting shops and head for The Office where a Thai curry in the pub garden is highly recommended. Moving on down Sydney Street and into Kensington Gardens, a bottle of beer on the Fringe Bar balcony will have you looking very stylish. Fight your way through the throngs on this pedestrianised street and turn right onto North Road before taking an immediate left into the French-style Dorset on Gardner Street. Fortified by a Kronenbourg and some moules stroll on down Gardner Street and Bond Street onto North Road for an expensive cocktail in Saqqara. Turn left out of there and pop into the Royal Pavillion Gardens to be awed before heading into the Suga Qube to stabilise your brain with a selection of vodkas. Head next down East Street or the Old Steine to the seafront. If you can resist the lure of the beach then go into the sprawling Prodigal or the

subterranean Ali Cats beneath it. Walk west along the Kings Road crunching on some rock before turning up West Street and calling into either the cheap Wetherspoons or the cool Standard before the long climb back up towards the station, passing the Clock Tower and nipping into the Polar Central for some modern bar action.

Hanover

A real treasure-trove of pub goodies await you providing you aren't afraid of a few hills. To help you out we've started the crawl at the top, so you can always get a taxi or a lift there!

Start off in the very pleasant The Walmer on Queen's Park Road and then head up the hill to The Hanover, the newest pub in the area. Then turn off and head down Southover Street, stopping almost immediately at the Pub With No Name where the food comes highly recommended. Now you could just head down Southover Street from here and call in at the Charles Napier, Dover Castle, The Geese Have Gone Over the Water, and The Greys, but we heartily recommend turning left off the road after the Dover Castle for a rewarding diversion. First head to the Constant Service on Islingwood Road and then head down that road to the classy Reservoir on Howard Road, before carrying on down Islingwood Road to the homely London Unity. After leaving here turn right and walk back to Southover Street to go in the Geese or the Greys. By now you will either be feeling sleepy or up for it. If it's the later then walk down to the Lewes Road and turn right to walk down to Phoenix Place to check out the bands that are sure to be on in the Free Butt.

Hove

Actually starting just within 'Brighton' near the end of Western Road this crawl then takes you over the border and on into Hove. Beginning at the Juggler with a friendly pint, then walk west along Western road to the Freemasons Arms for another pint or, more recklessly, a cocktail upstairs. Continue west along Western road and turn into Farm road and for a visit to the lively Cooper's Cask. This is the top rated pub on this crawl, so it's all downhill from here. Back to Western road and continue west through the square and onto Church road. Call in at the unusual Snafu 23 if its open and then continue on to the Greenhouse Effect where you may be entertained with some live music. On Westwards for an excellent beer in the Blind Busker, possibly sampling one of the extensive range of bottled Belgian beers. At First Avenue take a right and seek out the hidden but huge Hove Place and its extensive garden. Out of here and back onto Church road, then turn into Second Avenue to roll into the Hove Tin Drum for either a meal or to get thrown out. Then you have a decent walk along Church road to get to George Street. Take a right into this and have a very cheap pint in the Cliftonville Inn, a Wetherspoons boozer. Amble on up George street and into Goldstone Villas where you will come upon The Station for a final beer and possibly a pizza. You are now conveniently located for a train home from the nearby Hove station.

Kemptown

Starting out in the wilds of Kemptown and gradually bringing you into the welcoming arms of the centre of Brighton, this is the ideal crawl to get you up for a night dancing or possibly a curry. Start off with a pint or two in the entertainment centre of the Rock Inn on Rock Street then walk west to The Dragon on St. George's Road. Walk on along St. George's Road and if it is open then pop into the Bombay Bar for a quick one and maybe some live music. Move on down the road and turn into College Place for a pint in the Wellington. Then back to St. George's Road for a pint of locally brewed beer at the Hand in Hand. On towards town, you can't miss the Sidewinder, the highest rated pub in the St. James' Street area. Then turn off Upper St. James' Street into Upper Bedford Street for a pint in the pleasant Stag pub. Onward and downward to Rock Place, where you can have a beer or a canister of oxygen in the Brighton Rock. Out of there and back onto St. James' Street for the final run into town with a pint in the Ranelagh Arms and then another in the St. James Tavern. Then on into town if time and your constitution permits it.

West of the Station

This area is packed with quality pubs within very short range of each other. Resist the charms of the Grand Central and instead head down Surrey Street to line your stomach with a quality pint of real ale in the Evening Star. You can sample them first if you don't fancy a gamble! Then continue south onto North Gardens and the Caxton Arms. Double back on yourself from there and turn left to find The Eddy on Guildford street for a possible incident involving a shot of Absinthe. Now walk North along this street onto Guildford Road and an appointment in the Sussex Yeoman. If you are hungry then you could eat in here or have more traditional (but still excellent) pub grub across the road in the Battle of Trafalgar. You won't get any vinegar in here for your chips though as the pub prides itself on the quality of its beer and apparently vinegar makes beer go flat! Down Guildford Road and turn right at the bottom onto Buckingham Place. Up the hill and over the road into the Belle Vue, a bar that never seems as good as it should be. When coming out of here turn immediate left and left again into Chatham Place, which on a stroll by (possibly) Brighton's oldest petrol station leads you to the Zel pub, the Shakespear's Head. After a pint in here ask for directions to the Prestonville Arms or you will never find it. If you fancy going it alone then cross the street and head up Hamilton Road to this superb, but well hidden, pub. If you have achieved this mission then take up the next, which is to find the Marques of Exeter pub on Upper Hamilton road, where with any luck you will be treated to an Elvis Impersonator contest.

If after all this you are after a final challenge then head back into town and track down The Crescent on Clifton Hill. Good luck!

Ditchling Road

Not an area where a pub crawl is strongly recommended and the one we have put together here involves a fair old stroll which takes you into the Lewes Road area near the gyratory. The good news is that there are plenty of buses back into town from the end.
Commence drinking in the Druids Arms at the northern corner of the level on Ditchling road. Go up the hill from here and take a left at the lights onto Viaduct road and then another left down a little alley to the Rose Hill Tavern on Rose Hill Terrace. After a game of darts and a pint of Harveys take a left out of here, cross London road and go for a Fosters in the friendly semi-Australian theme dive of the Cobblers Thumb near the bottom of New England Road. Over the road, down a side street to Argyle Road and The Engineer and its (sometimes) cut-price beer. Here steel yourself for a hill and possibly getting lost. Turn right out to the pub, cross London Road again and continue up that street, you are now looking for Springfield Road and the superb pub-come-art-gallery of the Open House. Your legs will need the rest in one of the comfy settees because you are going to carry on up the hill to Ditchling road where you should turn right and drop in to The Roundhill. A quick livener here, then on and around the corner heading for Richmond Road and the Victoria, where depending on the atmosphere, you may want to stay for just a half or for the rest of the night!
From there it is a few minutes to the next pub. Continue on down Richmond Road to the bottom, turn right and then left, bringing you to the strange roundabout of the Gyratory. On the other side of this island from you is The Hub, where anyone over thirty will probably feel old, but by now you shouldn't care. Turn right out of The Hub onto the Lewes road and cross over to the laid back Gladstone where you can reflect on a job well done. I doubt you will make it out of there, but if you do you can walk on down the Lewes road back towards town before taking a right into St. Martin's street for an authentic and well deserved pint of Guinness at The Bugle.

Gay

This crawl takes you on a tour of the best Gay pubs in town, most of which are clustered to the East of the Old Steine. Start off early with the hectic Bulldog before walking down to the tiny Marine Tavern in Broad Street. Then wend your way down St. James' Street to the Steine, where you take a right and head away from the sea and into the welcoming Malborough Hotel. If you don't get distracted by the play that may be on upstairs then come out of there and walk back towards the seafront, but before you get there turn left into Steine Street and "Freddie Mercury's" pub, The Queen's Head, where there may be a cabaret show on. Round the corner into the earthy Aquarium before heading down to the seafront and into the rather cool Amsterdam. From there stroll down towards the pier to the new and flashy Charles St. to mull over your options. You could either go around the corner to the Revenge Club or you could head along Kings Road to Dr. Brighton's from where all the seafront clubs are accessible or take the longer stroll over to The Regency, past Churchill Square in Regency Mews.

Pub Drinking Games

These are games where the penalties for losing are that you are forced to drink quicker. The usual penalty is either to drink two fingers of your own drink (with two fingers being the measure of how much the level of your drink has to fall), or some amount of a penalty drink that a group of you are sharing. This amount could be two fingers, half or all of it, depending on what it is. Good penalty drinks are shots, especially tequila or vodka, bottles, pints, or possibly the dangerous old standby of a bit of what everyone is drinking, all mixed together in another glass!

Often these games are best played as a mixture so that people don't concentrate too much on a game to the detriment of the evening. A good mix is Mr. Thumbs, Left Handed-Right Handed Drinking and the Cigarette Game or Bunnies.

Mr Thumbs

An extremely simple game guaranteed to get everyone completely paranoid. Someone starts as Mr. Thumbs and all they have to do is put their thumb in a very visible position and keep it there, the edge of a table is the favoured position. As people in the group notice the thumb they have to do the same with theirs. This continues until only one person is left, who then has to carry out the drinking (or other) forfeit and then becomes the next Mr. Thumbs.

The Cigarette Game

To play this game you need a pint glass, a sheet of toilet paper, a cigarette and a coin, ideally a penny. I'm assuming here that smoking hasn't yet been banned in Brighton pubs! Wet the edge of the pint glass and stick the toilet paper to the top so that it completely covers the end of the glass. Now balance the coin in the middle. It should be well supported. Now light the cigarette and take turns burning holes in the toilet paper. Each hole must either not touch another hole or must burn a link of tissue paper which holds two holes together. The game ends when the coin falls in the glass and the person holding the cigarette carries out the forfeit.

Left Handed-Right Handed Drinking

Another very simple game, which requires only a reliable watch or clock. Whilst the minute hand of the clock is on the right hand side of the face players are only allowed to drink using their right hand. When the minute hand is on the left hand side of the clock players must drink with their left hand. Anyone caught drinking with the wrong hand must pay the penalty. If however someone is challenged as drinking and the challenge is incorrect then the challenger must pay the penalty. Its well worth watching out for which hand the person drinks with when they do pay the penalty!

Pub Golf

Ideally pub golf is based around a pub crawl. In each pub you count the number of swigs (shots) it takes to finish your pint. That is the player's score for that hole. Record the score and carry on to the next pub until you have completed the course. A variant is to have a different drink specified for each pub that all the players have to drink – if you are organised enough you could work out a par for each drink (a shot =1, etc). You'll have to agree between the players what the prize is for the lowest scoring round.

Spoof

Each player needs 3 coins. Each round the players secretly put 0-3 of the coins in their right hand. Then, going clockwise around the table the players must predict the total number of coins that are in the right hands. You cannot choose a number that someone else has already chosen in that round. If someone gets the number right then they are out. In the next round the person who predicted 2nd in the previous round starts the predicting. The game continues until only one person is left and then they must perform whatever forfeit was agreed at the start of the round. This game gets pretty tense when it is down to only two people in the final 'shoot out'.

Bunnies

The classic ridiculous pub drinking game. The players sit in a rough circle and one of them is nominated to start as the 'Bunny'. The 'Bunny' must waggle their hands on their head like a rabbit. The person to their left must waggle only their right hand on their head and the person to the right must only waggle their left hand. The 'Bunny' must then point at another player with both hands and that person is the new Bunny. If anyone reacts particularly slowly (usually the people on either side of the new Bunny) then they must pay the forfeit.

Fuzzy Duck

Another classic ridiculous pub drinking game. The players again sit in a rough circle and someone starts by saying 'Fuzzy Duck'. Play goes clockwise and players must keep saying 'Fuzzy Duck' until someone says 'Does he?', which changes the direction to anti-clockwise and everyone must then say 'Ducky Fuzz', until someone says 'Does he?' and the direction changes to clockwise. The game continues until someone says something other than 'Fuzzy Duck', 'Ducky Fuzz' or 'Does he?' when they must pay the forfeit. You can make the game harder by introducing words which mean that someone misses a go.

Banned Word Game

In this game each player proposes a word that is then banned for the rest of the game. If anyone says that word then they must pay the forfeit. This game is best played in conjunction with some other games.

THE CLUBS

Brighton Club Guide

This section gives a brief guide to Brighton clubs. Prices and descriptions could be totally wrong as they can change wildly.

Arc
Kings Road Arches on the seafront, 01273 770505
Beach bar becomes Club at night. Playing Disco/Funk/Soul or R'n'B/Rap/Ragga £8

Audio
Marine Parade, 01273 606906
Funk/Soul/Disco/House/Indie in a large club/bar with two distinct floors. £8.

Babylon Lounge
Kingsway
Playing House/Techno £7

The Beach
Kings Road Arches on the seafront, 01273 722272
Bar becomes huge open plan club at night. Plays classic club tunes or 70s/80s/90s. £10

BLo
West Street, Lanes, 01273 321692
R&B, Hip Hop & Garage. £6.

Brighton Gloucester
Gloucester Place, 01273 688011
No frills studenty place, Indie or School Disco £6.

Casablanca
Middle Street, Lanes. 01273 709710
Live funk jazz and latin in a cocktail of latin/Mexican cultures. £7.

Club Fuk
St. James's Street, 01273 695569
Small and gay, playing dance of all kinds. £6.

Club New York
Dyke Road, 01273 208678
Salsa, £4.

Concorde 2
Madeira Drive, 01273 606460
Live bands and big DJs, various prices around a tenner.

Core Club
Kings Road, Lanes, 01273 326848
Small crazy club playing an indie/pop/amusing mix. £4.

Creation
West Street, 01273 321628
Huge newish club that replaced the infamous Paradox. House/dance/party anthems. £8

Enigma
Ship Street, 01273 328439
Hip hop/garage/funk. £7.

Event 2
West Street, 01273 732627
Commercial dance and 70s/80s/90s anthems in the company of hen and stag dos. £7

Funky Buddha Lounge
Kings Road Arches (seafront), 01273 725541
Soul/funk/rare grooves in a pair of the arches. £10.

Funky Fish
Madeira Hotel, Maderia Drive, 01273 698331
The famous informal ex-Catfish club, playing Disco/funk/jazz/blues/soul, £5.

Gap Club
Western Road, Hove, 01273 203130
School disco/just plain disco, £6.

Hanbury Ballroom
St.George's Road, Kemptown, 01273 605789
Funk/soul/DJs/live music/unpredictable in a domed ex-mausoleum. £5.

Honey Club
Kings Road Arches (seafront), 01273 202807
Massive beach bar/club on the seafront plays techno house and trance. £9

Jazz Place
Ship Street, Lanes, 01273 328439
Tiny underground club playing (duh) jazz. £6.

Kookulb
Pool Valley, 01273 888000
'Late night venue and lounge bar' playing 'funky sexy house'. Fancy website! £8/£10

Ocean Rooms
Morley Street, 01273 699069
Award winning three-floor club playing disco, house, drum & bass. They tell us that the music policy is varied across the week and they "do not really do any cheesy nights"! £8

Pavilion Tavern
Castle Square, Lanes, 01273 827641
Usually packed low-budget late night drinking club above the Pav Tav. Playing indie, pop, retro, soul and disco classics. £5.

Po Na Na
East Street, Lanes, 0800 7837485
Chain bar with Turkish theme playing funk to a moneyed crowd. £6

Pool
Marine Parade, 01273 624091
Girly gay club with live music, house, techno, 70s/80s, indie, pop. £8

Pressure Point
Grand Parade, 01273 677800
Live bands and hip hop/reggae/drum & bass/house to a black t-shirt gang above the Pressure Point bar. £6.

Revenge
Old Steine, 01273 697569
Very large gay club with disco/dance/pop entertaining mainly men. £8

Snafu 23
Church Road, Hove, 01273 739399
DJs play hip hop/funk/house and this bar that becomes a club later. £5

Steamers
Kings Road, 01273 775775
Techno/rap/garage/house. £7

Volks
Madeira Drive, 01273 682828
House/techno/trance/hip hop on a two-floor club. £7

Zap
Kings Road Arches (seafront), 01273 202407
Cavernous dark maze with garage/hip hop/house/disco/anthems. Was briefly renamed 'Union' but returned to its original name. £10

THE REST

FARM
CASK ALES
UPSTAIRS BAR
TAVERN
UPSTAIRS AT THE FARM
Quality Cask Ales

Local Breweries and Beers

Brighton has only a couple of tiny breweries, but a number of breweries exist in the surrounding area. Most of the following are in Sussex. A lot of the following information is from www.quaffale.org.uk or www.brightoncamra.org.uk

1648 Brewery

East Hoathly's very own Village Brewery and Brew Pub. The Kings Head, in the centre of the village, is the primary outlet for the beer and the brewery can be found at the start of Mill Lane, just to the left of the pub. www.1648brewing.co.uk

Arundel Brewery Ltd

Opened in 1992. New owners in 1998, in an industrial unit south of Arundel. Many 'occasionals' are brewed (on sale for one month each) together with its award-winning mild. Possible outlets: The Swan, High Street, Arundel & The Maypole, Yapton.

Ballard's Brewery Ltd

Founded in July 1980 on Cumbers Farm, Trotton near Reigate. Purchased the Railway Inn, Elsted in 1985 and renamed in Ballards Pub and moved the brewery there. In 1988, with the need for extra space necessary, the pub was sold and the brewery moved to its current location, which despite the postal address, is actually in Sussex. A 10 barrel brewplant is used. Based in Nyewood. www.ballardsbrewery.org.uk

Regular outlets: various, including The Selden Arms, Worthing

Beard & Co. Ltd

Brewing from about 1740, this brewery was acquired by Thomas Beard in 1811. Brewing ceased in 1958, however the company retained its pubs. Initially beers were contract brewed by Harveys until 1986. By 1996 a Beard's branded beer was being brewed by Arundel. The remnants of Beard's were purchased by Greene King in July 1998

Custom Beers Ltd

Peter Skinner's five barrel brewery is on a farm site not far from Dark Star's. Apart from four regular beers, beer is brewed to order if you buy sufficient quantity - 'Think it, Drink it!'. There may be a small amount of bottling in the near future. Near Haywards Heath.

Dark Star Brewing Co. Ltd

Small 1 barrel brewery set up as Skinner's Ales in 1994 by Peter Skinner and Peter Halliday in the cellar of their pub, The Evening Star, Brighton. In 1995 they formed the Dark Star Brewing Company with Rob Jones (formerly with Pitfield Brewery) adding Dark Star (CAMRA Champion Beer of Britain 1987) and Rob's other beers alongside the Skinners range. Both companies names are used but should not be confused with 'Skinners Fine Cornish Ales' based in Truro. Over time the Skinner's brandname was dropped leaving all beers under the Dark Star name. In 2000 Peter Skinner left, later setting up Skinner's Custom Brews. In July 2001 a new 10 barrel plant started brewing in Ansty, near Haywards Heath.

Regular Outlets: Evening Star, Brighton; Stand Up Inn, Lindfield; Duke of Wellington, Shoreham; plus other free houses in the area

Fallen Angel Microbrewery

Brews only for bottling and appears at Farmers markets, Food Fairs and the like, locally. Have been going since the start of 2005. Based in Battle.
www.fallenangelbrewery.com

FILO Brewery

Started brewing in December 1985. The 5 barrel brewplant is home made from old dairy equipment. A major refurbishment of the plant took place during the summer of 2000. Based in Hastings.
Regular Outlet: FILO beers are generally only available at The First In, Last Out, Hastings.
www.thefilo.co.uk

The Gribble Brewery

The plant of the defunct Bosham Brewery was moved to the Gribble Inn, Oving, nr Chichester in the summer of 1987. Brewing ceased in 1989 but restarted in 1991 with the pub now being under the ownership of Hall & Woodhouse. A 4 barrel brewplant produces it's own beers independently but pays rent to Hall & Woodhouse.
Regular Outlets: The Gribble Inn is the main outlet for these beers but they can sometimes be found elsewhere now they are independent.
www.gribblebrewery.co.uk

Hammerpot

Opened in April 2005, based in The Vineries just south of the A27 at Poling..
www.hammerpot-brewery.co.uk

Harvey & Son (Lewes) Ltd

Founded in 1790, the current brewery was built in Lewes in 1881. Brewhouse capacity was doubled in 1985 from 25,000 to 50,000 barrels a year. Today, Harveys remains an independent, family company and is the main brewer of Sussex.
Regular Outlets: The brewery owns 43 pubs all of which sell real ale. The beer is available in a large number of Brighton freehouses.
www.harveys.org.uk

Hepworth & Co

Opened during the spring of 2001 by the ex-head brewer of Kings & Barnes in Horsham. This brewery has a modern bottling plant and contract bottles for many other brewers. www.thebeerstation.co.uk

Kemptown Brewery Co. Ltd

Based in the Hand in Hand pub in Kemptown, they claim to be the smallest brewpub in Britain. This pub started brewing in November 1989. A five barrel tower style brewplant is somehow shoehorned into the pub.
Regular Outlets: The Hand in Hand is the main outlet for these beers but several other pubs are currently supplied with beer.

King & Barnes Ltd

Formed from the merger of King & Sons, a maltsters set up in 1850, and G. H. Barnes & Co., a brewers dating back to 1800, in 1906 this family owned brewery survived until they were bought by Hall & Woodhouse in Spring 2000, with all production at Horsham ceasing. Sussex Bitter and Old Ale are brewed at Hall & Woodhouse, in Dorset. The last member of the King family actively involved in the company independently now brews in Horsham as WJ King & Co (Brewers).

WJ King & Co (Brewers)

Based in Horsham. This company was started at the end of May 2001 by Bill King, the last member of the King family to be actively involved with King & Barnes before the brewery was sold by the shareholders.

Rectory Ales Ltd

Started brewing in July 1996, based at White House Farm, Plumpton Green using a 1½ barrel brewplant. The brewery is run by Rev Godfrey Broster and was set up to provide a way of raising money towards the repair of three parish churches. By the end of 1996 the brewery had outgrown it location and moved to their present location in Streat Hill, near Hassocks, during the early months of 1997. A 5 barrel brewplant is used at the new location. Irregular Outlets: Evening Star, Brighton; The White Horse, Ditchling. www.rectory-ales.co.uk

Rother Valley Brewing Company

Brewing started in June 1993 using the 5 barrel brewplant formerly at Mr Cherry's Brewpub in St. Leonards-On-Sea. Only hops grown on the nearby hop farm were used. Based at Northiam, E. Sussex on the Kent border, with one tied house near Bodiam.

Weltons

Ray Welton has his own small brewery across the railway line from Hepworth's 'Beer Station', and supplies local pubs and festivals direct with his ever-changing range of beers, some brewed or badged for special occasions. Plans to brew 50 different beers during 2006 and one of his beers featured in Roger Protz's recent book '300 Beers to Try Before You Die'.

White Brewing Company

Husband and wife team David & Lesley White founded this small Bexhill brewery in 1995 as well as running a bar dispense equipment/service company and running bars at outdoor and special events. A small bottling plant has recently been installed so they can bottle their own plus other beers from small brewers in the area. About 20 outlets are supplied – plus summer events where their bars appear.

The Earth & Stars pub has organic beers on offer!

Local Pub Chains

A lot of Brighton pubs are tied to national breweries, but some local chains have arisen over the last ten years and now own large chunks of the city's bars. For a look at two of them, nip into the Easy Bar and the Western Front opposite each other off Churchill Square, these are run respectively by the rival companies C-Side and Zel.

There are also pubs from many national chains, such as; Hobgoblin, Hogshead, Firkin, Litten Tree, Walkabout, Wetherspoons and Yates'

C-Side

www.cside.co.uk

Definitely aimed at the younger drinking market and students, C-Side has expanded rapidly over the last nine years and owns pubs, bars and clubs. Here's what they say about themselves:

"C-Side is Brighton's largest, youngest and most rapidly expanding leisure company! Started in 1994 with one bar, The Squid, C-Side now operate over twenty venues in Brighton including five nightclubs, a restaurant, a fitness centre and many of Brighton's best bars and pubs.
C-Side employs over 350 people with an average employee age of just 23. The customer base is drawn from Brighton's two major universities and young professionals. The majority of C-Side venues sites are aimed at the 18-35 market.
C-Side has pioneered a new type of pub in Brighton – stylish well-designed premises offering an original product range, a funky atmosphere and some of the best music available. Many sites were previously derelict, run-down or undertrading and have been transformed into thriving refurbished businesses, providing a service that local customers want."
C-Side plan to expand into other towns……

Pubs: Arc, Beach, Bear, Easy Bar, Exchange, Fortunes of War, Gemini, Greens, Leek, Polars Central, East & West, Princess Victoria, Shark, Squid, Sumo

Golden Lion

www.goldenliongroup.co.uk

The Golden Lion group contains a rather strange mix of pubs from the down-to-earth Hove Place, through to the oldest pub in Brighton, The Cricketers, to one of the newest bars, the exclusive Ebony Room. It also has a number of pubs in the Sussex area, surrounding Brighton.

Pubs: Colonade Bar, Cricketers, Ebony Room, Golden Lion Tavern, Hove Place, Leo's Lounge, Lion D'Or,

Pleisure

www.pleisureltd.sagenet.co.uk/pubs.html

With eight pubs in Brighton, one in Lewes and one in London, Pleisure Ltd has not grown as fast as C-Side or Zel, but then it isn't really competing with them either. The Brighton pubs are largely modern versions of traditional pubs and all of them are have their own admirable qualities. Here's their history and philosophy:

"Well Pleisure Ltd - where to start? At the beginning I guess, way back in 1991. I suppose the best analogy is the phoenix from the ashes as the company has risen as a result of a father and son both being made redundant.
From the first venue opening in 1991 we have grown slowly but surely to the current compliment of 10 pubs. It has been our philosophy to maintain the feel of a family run business. Both myself and my father, Keith, have a history in the licensed trade and insist on the highest standards throughout.
It is our intention to continue to slowly develop the business and to allow our pubs to grow their own unique identities, (it is for this reason that we have become known as Brighton's pub alternative.) I believe that a pub should be a fun place to both be a customer and to work, a commitment that has come from a love of our industry."

Pubs: Aquarium, Dr. Brighton's, Great Eastern, Hectors House, Kings Arms, The Office, Pull & Pump, Saint James

Tin Drum

No website found

Are four pubs a chain? I'm not sure, but here it is anyway. These café/bars have proved popular enough to have gone from one to three very similar establishments in the same small city. This is a quote from one of the owners:

"All The Tin Drums are pretty unique in that they are successful cafe bars where the food element has remained important. Running a successful food venue in the city of Brighton & Hove is a tall order for any catering specialist so it is a remarkable achievement for Dave and Vicky because they are both trained as architects.
One day I just decided that I could design a contemporary bar far better myself. In 1998 I decided to put my money where my mouth was and opened the first Tin Drum."

Zel

www.zelnet.com

Zel or "The Connective" has gradually bought out a large number of Brighton pubs and then done them up into modern pub bars. Few pubs have not been improved by being 'Zelled', but they are not to everyone's tastes. Here is what the website says about themselves:

"There is much to celebrate about the world we live in, and there are few better places within which to celebrate than a pub. Our own enthusiasm for the lives we lead, our friendships, our freedom, our desires, all rise to the surface as our problems are pushed aside when we enter a pub conducive to celebration. But the possibilities for celebration extend far beyond the euphoria that can be gained from our immediate world. Our appreciation of art and culture, of the wider communities to which we belong and of the natural environment within which we live can all be excellent reasons to party if a pub is oriented towards making it so. And now a pub group with its heart in the city of Brighton UK, has created an ethos that aims to make it so."

"Ethos:
ZEL is an ethos aimed at stimulating the mind of the pub-goer as much as the taste buds. It is driven by a desire to create new ideas as much as to create wealth and is concerned with originality in everything and with the avoidance of homogenisation. It believes in operating a pub business in a non-corporate, balanced way that promotes positive impacts on culture, community and environment whilst limiting any negative impacts. It enjoys bringing people together and forming connections that improve the greater experience for everyone who comes into contact with a pub in the group.
ZEL's ultimate goal is to make pleasure a worthy pursuit."

You can decide if all this is bollocks or not by visiting one or more of the many Zel pubs.

Pubs: Cobblers Thumb, Earth & Stars, Fishbowl, Freebutt, Hanbury Ballroom, Juggler, Malborough, Mash Tun, Open House, Queens Head, Shakespears Head Western Front.

Pub Graveyard

This is a short list featuring the best and worst of the Brighton pubs that have been lost to renovation, demolition or just plain vanished!

Burlington

Now there was no need for this tragedy to happen. This excellent local was terminated, despite seeming popularity and an overall score of 65%. However, it was bought out, had its soul extracted and became the Polar East (now Duke of Norfolk).

Gull & Gerkin

A proper pub and well worth a visit if in the area, this one is well missed, its score of 61% reflecting a strong local following. It closed and re-opened as the Polar West after being completely gutted. Now it is only busy on Friday and Saturday nights.

Lamb & Flag

This appalling pub was surviving only from the scraps dropped by shoppers in Churchill Square and brain-dead local office workers. Its 22% rating from jurors was a solid prediction that this pub would die. The only problem was that it became the dreadful and soulless Easy Bar. Opposite the Lamb & Flag the equally dire Cranbourne became the actually quite good Western Front!

McClusky's

Hideous pub-come-nightclub on West Street, a real last resort bar with the dance floor as its only saving grace. Scoring a magnificent 23% there were no tears shed when this little beauty closed and reopened as a Wetherspoons.

Millers Arms

This pub had the best view from its beer garden of any pub in town. Unfortunately it was absolutely terrible apart from that, largely due to the customers. It scored a miserable 33% overall. Refurbished by the people behind the Full Moon as the aptly named 'Setting Sun' it became a hit and you are now privileged if you can get a seat in that garden at sunset.

Nan Tuks

A real loss with and overall score of 64%. This was Brighton's only gothic pub, featuring various interesting hidey holes and amazing horror film décor. A must for any budding mad scientist, a trip to the loo alone was a dangerous undertaking.
Transformed into the plastic monstrosity of the Biscuit Factory.

Pig in Paradise

At 32% this was a desolate pub, especially considering its prime location between the station and the beach. Frequented only by drunks and students it was no shock when it became the marginally better City of Brighton. This in turn was killed off to become the soulless but far better Polar Central.

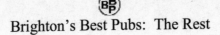

Tap & Spile
This trendy back street pub near the station was doing okay with a 52% overall score. Then it was inexplicably re-packaged as the awfully named 'Game of Life', but with no real change inside. This then became The Eddy, again with little noticeable change. Trendy pub became trendy pub became trendy pub. Why?

Windsor
An uninspiring town centre pub had a few regulars but this tiny minority of Brighton's population were the only ones to lament the passing of this sluggard of a pub. After a stunningly long period of time it then re-opened as the 'carbon neutral' totally green and organic pub, The Earth & Stars. Worth a visit now!

Updates

In the three years it has taken to compile this guide and rate the pubs we have on numerous occasions mistakenly concluded that we have correctly identified every pub in town. How wrong we have been. The number of pubs in the guide has risen from 218 to 242 to 263 to 285 to now 300. This is partly due to the continuing expansion of Brighton's drinking establishments – it seems that any (even wholly inappropriate) building can be converted into a pub/bar at the drop of a hat! We are now pretty sure that we have got the lot and only renaming or new pubs since going to print will be different to what is in this guide.

However, things do change, and especially so in Brighton. New pubs will be opened, current ones will close or be refurbished, management may change and detail will change quickly. Please write to us with any changes you see and they will be included in the next edition of this guide.

Our address is: Brightonpubs@yahoo.co.uk

Or check out the website: www.pubjury.co.uk

Disclaimer

Note that the scores and the descriptions given for the pubs are those determined by the jurors at the time of visiting. The publisher, editor and author of this book are not liable for any inaccuracies or insulting comments contained therein. If you would like to contest scores or comments, please write in and the pub will be re-visited and the points addressed.

THE DISTRACTIONS

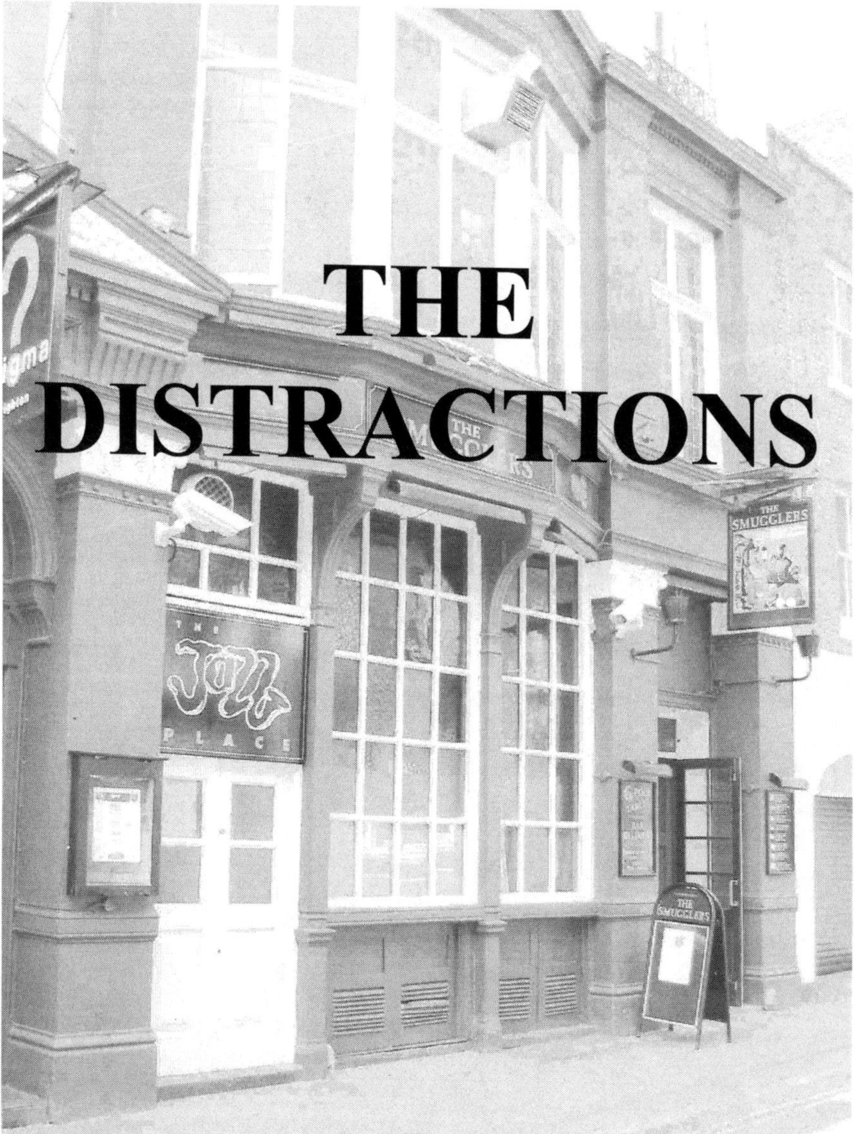

BBP

Brighton's Best Pubs: The Distractions

Boys Night Out Application Form

Name of Boyfriend/Fiancé/Husband:

I request permission for a leave of absence from the **highest authority** in my life for the following period:

Date: ______ Time of departure: ______ Time of return NOT to exceed: ______

Should permission be granted, I do solemnly swear to only visit the locations stated below, at the stated times. I agree to refrain from hitting on or flirting with other women. I shall not even speak to another female, except as expressly permitted in writing below. I will not turn off my mobile after two pints, nor shall I consume above the allowed volume of alcohol without first phoning for a taxi AND calling you for a verbal waiver of said alcohol allowance. I understand that even if permission is granted to go out, my girlfriend/fiancé/wife retains the right to be pissed off with me the following week for no valid reason whatsoever.

Alcohol allowed (units): Beer ______ Wine ______ Spirits ______ Total ______

Locations to be visited:

Location:	From:	To:
Location:	From:	To:
Location:	From:	To:

Females with whom conversation is permitted ______

IMPORTANT – STRIPPER CLAUSE: Notwithstanding the female contact permitted above, I promise to refrain from coming within one hundred (100) feet of a stripper or exotic dancer. Violation of this Stripper Clause shall be grounds for immediate termination of the relationship.

I acknowledge my position in life. I know who wears the trousers in our relationship, and I agree it's not me. I promise to abide by your rules & regulations. I understand that this is going to cost me a fortune in chocolates & flowers. You reserve the right to obtain and use my credit cards whenever you wish to do so. I hereby promise to take you to a Michael Bolton concert, should I not return home by the approved time. On my way home, I will not pick a fight with any stranger, nor shall I conduct in depth discussions with the said entity. Upon my return home, I promise not to urinate anywhere other than in the toilet. In addition, I will refrain from waking you up, breathing my vile breath in your face, and attempting to breed like a (drunken) rabbit.

I declare that to the best of my knowledge (of which I have none compared to my BETTER half), the above information is correct.

Signed - Boyfriend/Fiancé/Husband: ______

Request is: APPROVED ☐ DENIED ☐

This decision is not negotiable. If approved, cut permission slip below and carry at all times.

✂...

Permission for my boyfriend/fiancé/husband to be away for the following period of time:

Date: ______ Time of departure: ______ Time of return: ______

Signed – Girlfriend/Fiancé/Wife: ______

Pub Humour

MEDICAL WARNING!

The American Medical Association has declared that the long-term implications of drugs or medical procedures must be more fully considered. Over the past few years, more money has been spent on breast implants and Viagra than is spent on Alzheimer's disease research. It is now projected that by the year 2015 there will be fifty million people wandering around with huge breasts and large erections, who can't remember what to do with them.

MARKETING

For anyone who doesn't know what marketing is all about, or like to know more about marketing, you need to read this - carefully!

You see a gorgeous girl at a party. You go up to her and say, "I'm fantastic in bed." That's Direct Marketing.

You're at a party with a bunch of friends and see a gorgeous girl. One of your friends goes up to her and pointing at you says, "He's fantastic in bed." That's Advertising.

You see a gorgeous girl at a party. You go up to her and get her telephone number. The next day you call and say, "Hi, I'm fantastic in bed." That's Telemarketing.

You're at a party and see a gorgeous girl. You get up and straighten your tie, you walk up to her and pour her a drink. You open the door for her, pick up her bag after she drops it, offer her a ride, and then say, "By the way, I'm fantastic in bed." That's Public Relations.

You're at a party and see a gorgeous girl. She walks up to you and says, "I hear you're fantastic in bed." That's Brand Recognition.

DANCING

With all the sadness and trauma going on in the world at the moment, it is worth reflecting on the death of a very important person which went almost un-noticed last week. Larry La Prise, the man who wrote "The Hokey Kokey" died peacefully aged 83. The most traumatic part for his family was getting him into his coffin. They put his left leg in ... and things just started to go downhill from there.....!

NUNS

Sister Mary Katherine entered the Monastery of Silence.
The Priest said "Sister, this is a silent monastery. You are welcome here as long as you like, but you may not speak until I direct you to do so".

Sister Mary Katherine lived in the monastery for 5 years before the Priest said to her, "Sister Mary Katherine, you have been here for 5 years. You can speak two words. "Sister Mary Katherine said, "Hard bed."
"I'm sorry to hear that," the Priest said, "We will get you a better bed."

After another 5 years, Sister Mary Katherine was called by the Priest.
"You may say another two words, Sister Mary Katherine."
"Cold food," said Sister Mary Katherine, and the Priest assured her that the food would be better in the future.

On her 15th anniversary at the monastery, the Priest again called Sister Mary Katherine into his office. "You may say two words today."
"I quit," said Sister Mary Katherine.
"It's probably best", said the Priest, "You've done f*#k all else but moan since you got here."

TALKING DOG JOKE

A guy sees a sign in front of a house: "Talking Dog for Sale." He rings the bell and the owner tells him the dog is in the backyard. The guy goes into the backyard and sees a black mutt just sitting there. "You talk?" he asks.
"Sure do." the dog replies.
"So, what's your story?"
The dog looks up and says, "Well, I discovered my gift of talking pretty young and I wanted to help the government, so I told the MI5 about my gift and in no time they had me jetting from country to country, sitting in rooms with spies and world leaders, because no one figured a dog would be eavesdropping. I was one of their most valuable spies eight years running."
"The jetting around really tired me out, and I knew I wasn't getting any younger and I wanted to settle down. So I signed up for a job at the airport to do some undercover security work, mostly wandering near suspicious characters and listening in."
"I uncovered some incredible dealings there and was awarded a batch of medals. Had a wife, a mess of puppies and now I'm just retired."
The guy is amazed. He goes back in and asks the owner what he wants for the dog. The owner says, "Ten quid."
The guy says, "This dog is amazing. Why on earth are you selling him so cheap?"
"'Cause he's a bloody liar. He didn't do any of that."

PILOTS

You go to a party. How do you know which person is a pilot? They tell you.

After every flight, pilots complete a gripe sheet that conveys to the mechanics problems encountered with the aircraft during the flight that need repair or correction. The form is a piece of paper that the pilot completes, and then the mechanics read and correct the problem. They then respond in writing on the lower half of the form what remedial action was taken and the pilot reviews the gripe sheets before the next flight.
Never let it be said that ground crews and engineers lack a sense of humour. Here are some actual logged maintenance complaints and problems, as submitted by pilots, and the solution recorded by maintenance engineers.

P = The problem logged by the pilot.
S = The solution and action taken by the engineers.

P: Left inside main tire almost needs replacement.
S: Almost replaced left inside main tire.

P: Test flight OK, except autoland very rough.
S: Autoland not installed on this aircraft.

P: Something loose in cockpit.
S: Something tightened in cockpit.

P: Dead bugs on windshield.
S: Live bugs on back-order.

P: Autopilot in altitude-hold mode produces a 200 fpm descent.
S: Cannot reproduce problem on ground.

P: Evidence of leak on right main landing gear.
S: Evidence removed.

P: DME volume unbelievably loud.
S: DME volume set to more believable level.

P: Friction locks cause throttle levers to stick.
S: That's what they're there for.

P: IFF inoperative.
S: IFF always inoperative in OFF mode.

P: Suspected crack in windshield.
S: Suspect you're right.

P: Number 3 engine missing.
S: Engine found on right wing after brief search.

P: Aircraft handles funny.

S: Aircraft warned to straighten up, fly right, and be serious.

P: Target radar hums.
S: Reprogrammed target radar with words.

P: Mouse in cockpit.
S: Cat installed.

TOP EIGHT GEMS OF MILITARY WISDOM

1 - If the enemy is in range, so are you.
2 - Incoming fire has the right of way.
3 - Try to look unimportant, they may be low on ammo.
4 - Teamwork is essential; it gives the enemy someone else to shoot at.
5 - When the pin is pulled, Mr. Grenade is not our friend.
6 - If it's stupid but works, it isn't stupid.
7 - Never share a foxhole with anyone braver than you.
8 - A Purple Heart just proves that you were smart enough to think of a plan, stupid enough to try it, and lucky enough to survive.

YOUR HEALTH QUESTIONS ANSWERED…....

Q: I've heard that cardiovascular exercise can prolong life. Is this true?
A: Your heart is only good for so many beats, and that's it, don't piss them away on exercise. Everything wears out eventually. Speeding up your heart will not make you live longer; that's like saying you can extend the life of your car by driving it faster. Want to live longer? Take a nap.

Q: Should I cut down on meat and eat more fruits and vegetables?
A: You must grasp logistical efficiencies. What does a cow eat? Hay and corn. And what are these? Vegetables. So a steak is nothing more than an efficient mechanism of delivering vegetables to your system. Need grain? Eat chicken. Beef is also a good source of field grass (green leafy vegetable). And a pork chop can give you 100% of your recommended daily allowance of vegetable slop.

Q: Is beer or wine bad for me?
A: Look, it goes to the earlier point about fruits and vegetables. As we all know, scientists divide everything in the world into three categories: animal, mineral, and vegetable. We all know that beer and wine are not animal, and they are not on the periodic table of elements, so that only leaves one thing, right? My advice: Have a
burger and a beer and enjoy your liquid vegetables.

Q: How can I calculate my body/fat ratio?
A: Well, if you have a body, and you have body fat, your ratio is one to one. If you have two bodies, your ratio is two to one, etc.

Q: What are some of the advantages of participating in a regular exercise program?
A: Can't think of a single one, sorry. My philosophy is:
No Pain - Good.

Q: What's the secret to healthy eating?
A: Thicker gravy.
Q: If I stop smoking, will I live longer?
A: Nope. Smoking is a sign of individual expression and peace of mind.
If you stop, you'll probably stress yourself to death in record time.

Q: Aren't fried foods bad for you?
A: You're not listening. Foods are fried these days in vegetable oil. In fact, they're permeated in it. How could getting more vegetables be bad for you?

Q: Will sit-ups help prevent me from getting a little soft around the middle?
A: Definitely not! When you exercise a muscle, it gets bigger. You should only be doing sit-ups if you want a bigger stomach.

FOR MEN TIRED OF RECEIVING MALE-BASHING JOKES

How many men does it take to open a beer?
None. It should be opened by the time she brings it.

Why is a Laundromat a really bad place to pick up a woman? Because a woman who can't even afford a washing machine will probably never be able to support you.

I married Miss Right. I just didn't know her first name was Always.

I haven't spoken to my wife for 18 months: I don't like to interrupt her.

Scientists have discovered a food that diminishes a woman's sex drive by 90%.
It's called a Wedding Cake.

Marriage is a 3-ring circus: Engagement Ring, Wedding Ring, Suffering.

In the beginning, God created the earth and rested. Then God created Man and rested. Then God created Woman. Since then, neither God nor Man has rested.

Why do men die before their wives? They want to.

A beggar walked up to a well-dressed woman shopping on Oxford Street and said, "I haven't eaten anything for days."
She looked at him and said, "I wish I had your willpower."

Young Son: "Is it true, Dad, I heard that in some parts of Africa a man doesn't know his wife until he marries her?"
Dad: That happens in every country, son.

The most effective way to remember your wife's birthday is to forget it once.

Women will never be equal to men until they can walk down the street with a bald head and a beer gut, and still think they are beautiful.

INDIAN CURRY RHAPSODY (a la Queen style)

Naan, just killed a man
poppadom against his head
Had lime pickle now he's dead.
Naan, dinner's just begun
But now I'm gonna pass it all away.

Naan, ooh, ooh
Didn't mean to make you cry
Seen nothing yet just see the loo tomorrow
Curry on, curry on
Cause nothing really Madras.

Too late, my dinner's gone
Sends shivers down my spine
Rectum aching all the time
Goodbye onion bhaji, I've got to go
Gotta leave you all behind and use the loo.

Naan, ooh, ooh
This doopiaza is so mild
I sometimes wish we'd never come here at all. * guitar solo *

I see a little chicken tikka on the side
Rogan Josh, Rogan Josh, pass the chutney made of mango
Vindaloo does nicely
Very very spicy
Meat!

Byriani (Byriani)
Byriani (Byriani)
Byriani and a naan
(A vindaloo loo loo loo)

I've eaten balti, somebody help me
He's eaten balti, get him to the lavatory
Stand you well back
'Case the loo is quarantined...

Here it comes
There it goes
Technicolor yawn
I chunder
No!
It's coming up again
(There he goes)
I chunder, it's coming back again
(There he goes)
Coming back again (up again)

Here it comes again.
(No no no no no no NO)

On my knees, I'm on my knees
On his knees, Oh, there he goes
This vindaloo
Is about to wreck my guts
Poor me.. poor me...poor meee! * guitar
solo *

So you think you can chunder and then feel alright?
So you try to eat curry and drink beer all night?
Oh maybe, But now you'll puke like a baby
Just had to come out
It just had to come right out in here. * guitar solo *

Korma, sag or bhuna
bhaji, balti or naan
Nothing really madras
Nothing really madras
To meee....

TOP 7 SEX JOKES

1. A young man walks up and sits down at the bar. "What can I get you?" the bartender inquires. "I want 6 shots of Jagermeister," responded the young man.
"6 shots?!? Are you celebrating something?"
"Yeah, my first blowjob."
"Well, in that case, let me give you a 7th on the house."
"No offence, sir. But if 6 shots won't get rid of the taste, nothing will."

2. A businessman boards a flight and is lucky enough to be seated next to an absolutely gorgeous woman. They exchange brief hellos and he notices she is reading a manual about sexual statistics. He asks her about it and she replies, "This is a very interesting book about sexual statistics. It identifies that American Indians have the longest average penis and Polish men have the biggest average diameter. By the way, my name is Kim. What's yours?"
He coolly replies, "Tonto Kawalski, nice to meet you."

3. One night, as a couple lay down for bed, the husband gently taps his wife on the shoulder and starts rubbing her arm. The wife turns over and says: "I'm sorry honey, I've got a gynaecologist appointment tomorrow and I want to stay fresh." The husband, rejected, turns over and tries to sleep. A few minutes later, he rolls back over and taps his wife again. This time he whispers in her ear: "Do you have a dentist appointment tomorrow too?"

4. Bill worked in a pickle factory. He had been employed there for a number of years when he came home one day to confess to his wife that he had a terrible compulsion. He had an urge to stick his penis into the pickle slicer. His wife suggested that he should see a

sex therapist to talk about it, but Bill indicated that he'd be too embarrassed. He vowed to overcome the compulsion on his own. One day a few weeks later, Bill came home absolutely ashen. His wife could see at once that something was seriously wrong. "What's wrong, Bill?" she asked. "Do you remember that I told you how I had this tremendous urge to put my penis into the pickle slicer?" "Oh, Bill, you didn't.", "Yes, I did." "My God, Bill, what happened?" "I got fired."
"No, Bill. I mean, what happened with the pickle slicer?" "Oh...she got fired too."

5. A guy walks into a bar with a pet alligator by his side. He puts the alligator up on the bar. He turns to the astonished patrons. "I'll make you a deal. I'll open this alligator's mouth and place my genitals inside. Then the gator will close his mouth for one minute. He'll then open his mouth and I'll remove my unit unscathed. In return for witnessing this spectacle, each of you will buy me a drink." The crowd murmured their approval. The man stood up on the bar, dropped his trousers, and placed his privates in the alligator's open mouth. The gator closed his mouth as the crowd gasped. After a minute, the man grabbed a beer bottle and rapped the alligator hard on the top of its head. The gator opened his mouth and the man removed his genitals unscathed as promised. The crowd cheered and the first of his free drinks were delivered. The man stood up again and made another offer. "I'll pay anyone £100 who's willing to give it a try". A hush fell over the crowd. After a while, a hand went up in the back of the bar. A woman timidly spoke up. "I'll try, but you have to promise not to hit me on the head with the beer bottle".

6. There was this couple who had been married for 50 years. They were sitting at the breakfast table one morning when the old gentleman said to his wife, "Just think, honey, we've been married for 50 years." "Yeah," she replied, "Just think, fifty years ago we were sitting here at this breakfast table together." "I know," the old man said, "We were probably sitting here naked as jaybirds fifty years ago." "Well," Granny snickered, "What do you say...should we get naked?" So the two stripped to the buff and sat down at the table. "You know, honey," the little old lady breathlessly replied, "My nipples are as hot for you today as they were fifty years ago."
"I wouldn't be surprised," replied Gramps. "One's in your coffee and the other is in your porridge!!!!

7. A woman meets a top bloke in a bar. They talk, they connect, they end up leaving together. They get back to his place, and as he shows her around his apartment, she notices that his bedroom is completely packed with sweet cuddly teddy bears. Hundreds of cute small bears on a shelf all the way along the floor, cuddly medium-sized ones on a shelf a little higher, and huge enormous bears on the top shelf along the wall.
The woman is surprised that this guy would have a collection of teddy bears, especially one that's so extensive, but she decides not to mention this to him, and actually is quite impressed by his sensitive side. She turns to him... they kiss... and then they rip each other's clothes off and make hot steamy love.
After an intense night of passion with this sensitive guy, they are lying there together in the afterglow, the woman rolls over and smiling, asks, "Well, how was it?"
The guy says, "Help yourself to any prize from the bottom shelf."

BUILDING MARRIAGE CAPITAL.......

For thousands of years, men have tried to understand the rules when dealing with women. Finally, this merit/demerit guide will help you to understand just how it works. In the world of romance, a single rule applies: MAKE THE WOMAN HAPPY:

Do something she likes, and you get points. Do something she dislikes and points are subtracted. You don't get any points for doing something she expects. Sorry, that's how the games played. Here is a guide to the points system:

SIMPLE DUTIES:

You make the bed...+1
You make the bed, but forget to add the decorative pillows .... -5
You throw the bedspread over rumpled sheets......................-1
You leave the toilet seat up...................................-15
You replace the toilet paper roll when it is empty.............. 0
When the toilet paper roll is barren, you resort to Kleenex ...... -1
When the Kleenex runs out you use the next bathroom............ -2
You go out to buy her extra-light panty liners with wings .... +5
in the snow.. +8
but return with beer..-5
and no liners..-25
You check out a suspicious noise at night....................... 0
You check out a suspicious noise and it is nothing.............. 0
You check out a suspicious noise and it is something........... +5
You pummel it with a six iron................................ +10
It's her cat.. -40

AT THE PARTY

You stay by her side the entire party......................... 0
You stay by her side for a while, then leave to chat with a college drinking buddy...................................... -2
named Tiffany.. -4
Tiffany is a lap dancer..................................... -10
with breast implants.. -18

HER BIRTHDAY

You remember her birthday.................................. 0
You buy a card and flowers.................................. +10
You take her out to dinner.................................. +15
You take her out to dinner and it's not a sports bar......... +1
Okay, it is a sports bar.................................. -10
And it's all-you-can-eat night.............................. -25
It's a sports bar, it's all-you-can-eat night, and your face is painted the colors of your favorite team........ -10

A NIGHT OUT WITH THE BOYS

Go with a pal... 0
The pal is happily married.................................. +25
The pal is single.. -7
He drives a Ferrari... -10
With a personalized license plate (GR8NBED).................. –50

A NIGHT OUT WITH HER

You take her to a movie..................................... +5
You take her to a movie she likes........................... +15
You take her to a movie you hate............................ +30
You take her to a movie you like............................ -5
It's called Death Cop 3..................................... -20
Which features Cyborg that eat humans....................... -50
You lied and said it was a foreign film about orphans .... -15

YOUR PHYSIQUE

You develop a noticeable pot belly........................... -15
You develop a noticeable pot belly and start exercising to get rid of it ....+10
You develop a noticeable pot belly and resort to loose jeans and baggy Hawaiian shirts............................. -30
You say, "It doesn't matter, you have one too."................ -800

THE BIG QUESTION

She asks, "Does this dress make me look fat?"
You hesitate in responding.................................. -10
You reply "Where?"... -35
You reply "No, I think it's your ass"......................... -100
Any other response... -20

COMMUNICATION

When she wants to talk about a problem:
You listen, displaying a concerned expression..................+10
You listen for over 30 minutes................................ +25
You relate to her problem and share a similar experience .... +50
Your mind wanders to sports and you suddenly hear her saying
"Well, what do you think I should do?"......................... -50
You listen for more than 30 minutes without looking at the TV.... +100
She realizes this is because you have fallen asleep........... –200

WISE SAYINGS FROM THE MAN AT THE BAR

1. Triangular sandwiches taste better than square ones.
2. At the end of every party there is always a girl crying.
3. One of the most awkward things that can happen in a pub is when your pint-to-toilet cycle gets synchronised with a complete stranger.
4. You've never quite sure whether it's OK to eat green crisps.
5. Everyone who grew up in the 80's has entered the digits 55378008 into a calculator.
6. Reading when you're drunk is horrible.
7. Sharpening a pencil with a knife makes you feel really manly.
8. You're never quite sure whether it's against the law or not to have a fire in your back garden.
9. Nobody ever dares make cup-a-soup in a bowl.
10. You never know where to look when eating a banana.
11. Its impossible to describe the smell of a wet cat.
12. Prodding a fire with a stick makes you feel manly.
13. Rummaging in an overgrown garden will always turn up a bouncy ball.
14. You always feel a bit scared when stroking horses.
15. Everyone always remembers the day a dog ran into your school.
16. The most embarrassing thing you can do as schoolchild is to call your teacher mum or dad.
17. The smaller the monkey the more it looks like it would kill you at the first given opportunity.
18. Some days you see lots of people on crutches.
19. Every bloke has at some stage while taking a pee flushed half way through and then raced against the flush.
20. Old women with mobile phones look wrong!
21. Its impossible to look cool whilst picking up a Frisbee.
22. Driving through a tunnel makes you feel excited.
23. You never ever run out of salt.
24. Old ladies can eat more than you think.
25. You can't respect a man who carries a dog.
26. There's no panic like the panic you momentarily feel when you've got your hand or head stuck in something.
27. No one knows the origins of their metal coat hangers.
28. Despite constant warning, you have never met anybody who has had their arm broken by a swan.
29. The most painful household incident is wearing socks and stepping on an upturned plug.
30. People who don't drive slam car doors too hard
31. You've turned into your dad the day you put aside a thin piece of wood specifically to stir paint with.
32. Everyone had an uncle who tried to steal their nose.
33. Bricks are horrible to carry.
34. In every plate of chips there is a bad chip.

Hangover Rating System

1-Star Hangover (*)

No pain. No real feeling of illness.
Your sleep last night was a mere disco nap that is giving you a whole lot of misplaced energy. Be glad that you are able to function relatively well.
However, you are still parched. You can drink 10 pints of water and still feel this way.
Even vegetarians are craving a bacon sarny with brown sauce.

2-Star Hangover (**)

No pain. Something is definitely amiss.
You may look okay but you have the attention span and mental capacity of a staple gun.
The coffee you chug to try and remain focused is only acerbating your rumbling gut, which is craving nothing but dry toast.
Last night has wreaked havoc on your bowels and even though you have a nice demeanor about the office, you are costing your employer valuable money because all you really can handle is surfing internet junk and writing social e-mails.

3-Star Hangover (***)

Slight headache. Stomach feels crappy.
You are definitely a space shot and so not productive.
Anytime a girl walks by you gag because her perfume reminds you of the tequila shots you did with your alcoholic friends at 1:45 a.m.
Life would be better right now if you were in your bed with a dozen donuts watching the MTV.
You've had 4 cups of coffee, a gallon of water, 3 Ribenas and a liter of coke - yet you haven't peed once.

4-Star Hangover (****)

Life sucks. Your head is throbbing and you can't speak too quickly or else you might puke.
Your boss has already lambasted you for being late and has given you a lecture for reeking of booze.
You wore nice clothes, but that can't hide the fact that you missed an oh-so crucial spot shaving, (girls, it looks like you put your make-up on while riding the bumper cars). Your teeth have sweaters, your eyes look like one big vein and your hair style makes you look like a reject from Grange Hill, '76.
You would shoot your mother for one or all of the following -

1. the clock to strike 6pm
2. the entire appetizer list from TGI Fridays
3. a time machine so you could go back and NOT have gone out the night before.

5-Star Hangover (*****), AKA Dante's 4th Circle of Hell.

You have a second heartbeat in your head that is actually annoying the employee who sits at the next desk.
Vodka vapor is seeping out of every pour and making you dizzy.
You still have toothpaste crust in the corners of your mouth from brushing your teeth.
Your body has lost the ability to generate saliva, so your tongue is suffocating you.
You'd cry but that would take the last of the moisture left in your body.
Death seems pretty good right now.
Your boss doesn't even get mad at you and your co-workers think that your dog just died because you look so pathetic.
You should have called in sick because, let's face it, all you can manage to do is bitch about your state - which is a mystery to you because you definitely don't remember who you were with, where you were, what you drank and why there is a stranger still sleeping in your bed, unaccompanied, at your house. The only thing you can do is smoke and pass out.
It's when you wake up a few hours later with a lesser star hangover that you eat a large pizza, an order of sweet and sour Chicken, a pot noodle and a batch fun size Mars bars.

6-Star Hangover (******) otherwise known as ultimate doom

You wake up on your bathroom floor fully dressed.
For about 2 seconds you look at the ceiling, wondering if the cool refreshing feeling on your cheek is the bathroom tile or your vomit from 5 hours ago.
You hear your roommate scampering around you, walking over you like you are a chalk-lined homicide. It is amazing how your roommate was as drunk as you, but somehow manages to get up before you the next morning.
You try to lift your head - Not an option.
You crawl pathetically toward the bowl. You look in it, and it looks like a cherry pie is floating in a pool of orangeade.
Yet that isn't what makes you gag. It is when you turn your head too quickly only to smell the funk of 13 packs of cigarettes in your hair, and suddenly you realize you weren't smoking ultra lights...some jackass handed you a Camel, and you smoked 3 of them like it was your second full time job.
You look in the mirror (you are a machosist at this point) only to see remnants of the stamp "Ready to Rock" faintly atop your forehead...that explains the stamp on the back of your hand that has magically appeared on your forehead by alcoholic osmosis.
You have to be in work in T-minus 14 minutes and 32 seconds and the only thing you can think of wearing is your hello kitty pajama bottoms, that damn cricket jumper from college, and your slippers.
Suddenly you realize sanctuary is only a sick day away...then you remember that 8:30 meeting.

Learned Quotes For The Beer Drinker

"Sometimes when I reflect back on all the beer I drink I feel shamed. Then I look into the glass and think about the workers in the brewery and all of their hopes and dreams. If I didn't drink this beer, they might be out of work and their dreams would be shattered. Then I say to myself, "It is better that I drink this beer and let their dreams come true than be selfish and worry about my liver." ~ Jack Handy

~~~~~~~~~~~~~~~~~~~~~~~~

"I feel sorry for people who don't drink. When they wake up in the morning, that's as good as they're going to feel all day. "
~Frank Sinatra

~~~~~~~~~~~~~~~~~~~~~~~~

"An intelligent man is sometimes forced to be drunk to spend time with his fools."
~ Ernest Hemingway

~~~~~~~~~~~~~~~~~~~~~~~~

"When I read about the evils of drinking, I gave up reading."
~ Henny Youngman

~~~~~~~~~~~~~~~~~~~~~~~~

"24 hours in a day, 24 beers in a case. Coincidence? I think not."
~ Stephen Wright

~~~~~~~~~~~~~~~~~~~~~~~~

"When we drink, we get drunk. When we get drunk, we fall asleep. When we fall asleep, we commit no sin. When we commit no sin, we go to heaven. Sooooo, let's all get drunk and go to heaven!" ~ Brian O'Rourke

~~~~~~~~~~~~~~~~~~~~~~~~

"Beer is proof that God loves us and wants us to be happy."
~ Benjamin Franklin

~~~~~~~~~~~~~~~~~~~~~~~~

"Without question, the greatest invention in the history of mankind is beer. Oh, I grant you that the wheel was also a fine invention, but the wheel does not go nearly as well with pizza." ~ Dave Barry

~~~~~~~~~~~~~~~~~~~~~~~~

BEER: HELPING UGLY PEOPLE HAVE SEX SINCE 3000 B.C.!!!

~~~~~~~~~~~~~~~~~~~~~~~~

Remember "I" before "E", except in Budweiser.

~~~~~~~~~~~~~~~~~~~~~~~~

To some it's a six-pack, to me it's a Support Group. Salvation in a can!

~~~~~~~~~~~~~~~~~~~~~~~~

And saving the best for last:
One afternoon at Cheers, Cliff Clavin was explaining the Buffalo Theory to his buddy Norm. Here's how it went: "Well ya see, Norm, it's like this... A herd of buffalo can only move as fast as the slowest buffalo. And when the herd is hunted, it is the slowest and weakest ones at the back that are killed first.
This natural selection is good for the herd as a whole, because the general speed and health of the whole group keeps improving by the regular killing of the weakest members. In much the same way, the human brain can only operate as fast as the slowest brain cells. Excessive intake of alcohol, as we know, kills brain cells. But naturally, it attacks the slowest and weakest brain cells first. In this way, regular consumption of beer eliminates the weaker brain cells, making the brain a faster and more efficient machine. That's why you always feel smarter after a few beers."
~~~~~~~~~~~~~~~~~~~~~~~~

Puzzles

1. A murderer is condemned to death. He has to choose between three rooms. The first is full of raging fires, the second is full of assassins with loaded guns, and the third is full of lions that haven't eaten in 3 years. Which room is safest for him?

2. A woman shoots her husband. Then she holds him under water for over ten minutes. Finally, she hangs him. But 5 minutes later they both go out together and enjoy a wonderful dinner together. How can this be?

3. There are two plastic jugs filled with water. How could you all the water into a barrel, without using the jugs or any dividers, and still tell which water came from which jug?

4. What is black when you buy it, red when you use it, and gray when you throw it away?

5. Can you name three consecutive days without using the words Monday, Tuesday, Wednesday, Thursday, Friday, Saturday, or Sunday?

6. This is an unusual paragraph.
I'm curious how quickly you can find out what is so unusual about it? It looks so plain you would think nothing was wrong with it! In fact, nothing is wrong with it! It is unusual though. Study it, and think about it, but you still may not find anything odd. But if you work at it a bit, you might find out! Try to do so without any coaching!

Brainteaser

This puzzle is supposed to have been written by Einstein. He said that 98% of the people in the world cannot solve it. Personally I think that is probably rubbish (the Einstein bit), but its quite good! Could you be among the other 2%?

- There are 5 houses, each a different colour
- In each house lives a person of a different nationality
- These five owners all drink a certain beverage, smoke a certain brand of cigar and keep a certain pet
- No owner has the same pet, smokes the same brand of cigar or drinks the same drink as another owner

1. The Briton lives in a red house
2. The Swede keeps dogs as pets
3. The Dane drinks tea
4. The green house is on the directly to the left of the white
5. The green house owner drinks coffee
6. The person who smokes Pall Mall rears birds
7. The owner of the yellow house smokes Dunhill
8. The man living in the house right in the centre drinks milk
9. The Norwegian lives in the first house
10. The man who smokes Blend lives next to the one who keeps cats
11. The man who keeps horses lives next to the man who smokes Dunhill
12. The owner who smokes Blue Master drinks beer
13. The German smokes Prince
14. The Norwegian lives next to the blue house
15. The man who smokes Blend has a neighbour who drinks water

The question is: WHO KEEPS FISH?

Puzzle Answers

1. The third. Lions that haven't eaten in three years are dead.
2. The woman was a photographer. She shot a picture of her husband, developed it, and hung it up to dry.
3. Freeze them first. Take them out of the jugs and put the ice in the barrel. You will be able to tell which water came from which jug.
4. The answer is Charcoal. In Homer Simpson's words: hmmmm...Barbecue.
5. Sure you can: Yesterday, Today, and Tomorrow!
6. The letter "e", which is the most common letter in the English language, does not appear once in the long paragraph.

Brainteaser Answer

The German keeps fish.